# HANDGUN
# TRAINING

## PRACTICE DRILLS
## FOR DEFENSIVE
## SHOOTING

GRANT
CUNNINGHAM

Published by

Gun Digest® Books, an imprint of F+W Media, Inc.
Krause Publications • 700 East State Street • Iola, WI 54990-0001
715-445-2214 • 888-457-2873
www.krausebooks.com

To order books or other products call toll-free 1-800-258-0929
or visit us online at www.gundigeststore.com

ISBN-13: 978-1-4402-4492-6
ISBN-10: 1-4402-4492-8

Designed by Sharon Bartsch
Edited by Corrina Peterson

Printed in China

10 9 8 7 6 5 4 3 2 1

# TABLE OF CONTENTS

# ACKNOWLEDGEMENTS

There are many training drills used by defensive shooting instructors, and they get passed around and often modified as they make their way amongst the community. Very few of them are attributable to a single person or survive in their original form, but rather end up belonging to the whole community. I've made an effort to attribute specific drills to the people I thought responsible, but even those drills which I concocted myself are in fact compilations of ideas from others and may go back years (if not decades).

Because of this "melting pot" of influences and ideas, I think it appropriate to thank those who not only invented drills but who have inspired in some way what you see in this book. In no particular order, I'd like to recognize and thank Georges Rahbani, Massad Ayoob, Rob Pincus, Claude Werner, Paul Carlson, Greg Ellifritz, Marty Hayes, Paul Gomez, Clyde Caceres, and Mike Seeklander for their inspiration over the years. Even if they didn't actually develop something in these pages, they certainly exposed me to ideas and, in some way, at some time, influenced how I look at defensive training. They (and others I've no doubt forgotten to add) have had some input into this book — whether they realize it or not.

# CHAPTER ONE

# THE TROUBLE WITH SHOOTING DRILLS

**The perceived need to make classes 'exciting' has produced many drills of dubious value to defensive training.**

When shooting instructors get together, a common topic of conversation is shooting drills. Everyone wants to find a new, exciting drill for their students so their curriculum is fresh and fun. They're always looking for difficult shooting challenges or drills from more famous instructors to give their programs a boost. The result is that a lot of shooting drills get made up and shared without any real purpose; sometimes, it seems as though the drills were suggested by ammunition makers keen on selling more product.

The problem with many of these drills is that they may not teach the defensive shooting student anything about the actual task of defensive shooting — more specifically, the private citizen who needs to defend himself or herself from a violent attack. There are many drills I've shot in my life that were a lot of fun, but weren't really germane to the idea of using a gun to defend my life.

When I look for a new drill, I'm not necessarily looking to have fun; that's just a byproduct, and if it works out that way so much the better! In general terms, I'm looking for a drill that will teach me something, or allow me to practice something I already

**Remember why we're training: to defend ourselves (or our loved ones) against a lethal attack.**

know (and already know to be important to the job of defending myself with that gun), or that gives me a way to judge how well I'm doing that job. If I'm going to expend my time, effort, ammunition, and money going to the range, I want to get something out of it.

That doesn't include some fuzzy, generalized goal of "becoming a better shooter" or "improving my gunhandling," either. Whether learning, practicing, or evaluating, I'm looking for my practice routine to do very specific things that are directly related to self defense. For instance, "improved marksmanship" isn't a goal I'd use (and won't use in this book); "practicing my ability to control multiple, realistic strings of fire" is a goal. Another might be "evaluating my skill at moving off the line of attack while drawing my gun to an accurate first-round hit." Still another might be "practicing my shot-to-shot assessment," or perhaps "how to quickly retrieve my defensive pistol from a quick-access safe and make it ready to use." Those are the kinds of goals I have when I go to the range.

"Becoming a better shooter" isn't relevant; becoming a better *defensive* shooter is. The only way to do that is to understand the tasks a defensive shooter needs to accomplish, and then find (or design) drills that teach or test the specific skills needed to perform

those tasks.

Now if the resulting drill just happens to be fun to shoot, so much the better!

## WHAT MAKES THIS BOOK (AND THESE DRILLS) DIFFERENT?

The drills in this book are all focused on helping you to develop specific skills that are valuable in defensive shooting. Every drill has been picked to address a skill or a need, and more importantly each one carries of an explanation of the what and the why — rather than just "here's something cool to try!"

These are really task-oriented practice routines, in the sense that they're based on the kinds of things real people do (or need to do) when actually faced with a deadly threat (a threat to which shooting is the correct response). I'm indebted to the work of people like Claude Werner, who has done extensive research into the kinds of tasks people end up performing in defensive shootings. From his (and other's) list of probabilities, we can look at what we're likely to need to do and choose/create drills that address exactly those needs.

That's what you'll find in the rest of this book.

# CHAPTER TWO

# THE THINGS WE WANT TO PRACTICE

The shooting drills presented in this book are task-oriented; they're designed to provide practice opportunities for the tasks most likely required in an actual defensive shooting. What, then, are the things we need to practice?

This is a common question in the defensive shooting world. Many people have tried to answer it but, unfortunately, a dispassionate, fact-based answer is difficult to come by. This is because most people answer the question not from the kind of research done by leaders in the field like Claude Werner and Tom Givens, but from biases based on their own shooting activities or careers.

Some people come with an equipment bias: they do certain things because they like the equipment,

then search for ways in which to use that equipment and do drills which validate their equipment selections. Certain types of gear will dictate that you do things a certain way, or that you use them instead of something more suitable. An equipment bias limits what you'll do (or can do or can train) to things that fit what you have, rather than making what you have fit the task at hand.

Take, for instance, a flashlight mounted on a handgun. There are certainly uses for such devices, but they're pretty specific and are never a substitute for other forms of illumination. Too many folks, however, will practice their "low light" drills with these exclusively, to the detriment of actually being able to use better-suited and more common illumina-

**An equipment bias causes you to try to tailor your training around your gear, trying to find situations or make up techniques just to be able to utilize that equipment.**

**A competition bias too often leads to taking shortcuts in technique (or equipment) selection just to get a better score.**

tion tools — things like handheld flashlights (or even room light switches!). This particular gear bias results in low-light drills being designed that don't accurately reflect the conditions under which supplementary lighting might really be needed. The "bump in the night" that results in your muzzle sweeping your teenage child coming home past his bedtime might be the unfortunate result of such an equipment bias.

Equipment isn't the only bias people have, of course. Some come to the discussion with a source bias: because a drill or technique comes from an authoritative or charismatic figure, people often feel compelled to practice and promote it even though it may not fit the context under which it will be used. The implicit correctness which we perceive because of the source's pedigree is a form of the logical fallacy "appeal to authority," where the merits of the proposal aren't discussed because of the unimpeachable nature of the source. Many of the military-inspired training routines that have nothing to do with private sector defensive shooting come from source bias.

There is also a scoring bias: we practice to improve ourselves by some objective measure, even if that measure has no real bearing on our ability to defend ourselves. This is heavily prevalent in the shooting world, owing to the number of competition shooters who have moved into the training realm over the years. (This is not to discount the value of competition as a test bed for new techniques and equipment, you

understand, only to put their interest in objective scoring into perspective.)

What you'll find in this book are task-oriented drills that are competency-based, allowing you to progress at the rate that's right for you.

## WHAT ARE THE TASKS WE NEED TO PRACTICE?

A shooting response to a lethal threat is a complex series of observations and reactions. There are a number of skills involved in a successful response, and luckily for us our innate abilities developed over millennia help us tremendously. Learning to use a specific tool like a firearm, however, is not an innate or "instinctive" skill — it's something we learn to do in concert with what we already know and do.

So, what are the kinds of things you need to train and practice? In no particular order, here are just a few of the things you might need to be able to do quickly and efficiently:

- Get a proper grasp on the gun
- Bring the gun from the holster to the target
- Decide if and when you need to shoot, and when you need to stop shooting
- Retrieve the pistol from a storage device
- Use the gun in concert with illumination of some type
- Reload the gun when it runs out of ammunition
- Clear a malfunction
- Recognize the level of precision to which you need to shoot
- Deliver that level of precision on target
- Deal with more than one attacker
- Shoot rapid, multiple rounds to an appropriate level of precision
- Shoot one-handed

Of course there's a lot more, but this should give you an idea of what this concept of "task-oriented" training means: practicing those things that are actually needed in a defensive shooting.

Foundational skills, like getting the gun out of the holster efficiently, are the basis of defensive shooting.

# CHAPTER THREE

# THE POWER OF VISUALIZATION

The value of visualization as a teaching tool is well established. Visualization has been used in fields as disparate as basketball and mathematics, and nearly everything else in between, to elicit better performance.

In the realm of defensive shooting, visualization is a great way to allow us to train and practice the circumstances of an actual event. The only other way to get close to what you'll actually need to do in a defensive shooting is to participate in force-on-force training (FOF, aka 'scenario training' or 'reality based training') with simulated ammunition and others playing the role of attackers. While FOF is a great training tool, it requires specialized equipment (some of which isn't available to non-certified personnel), careful scripting, and well-trained role-players. All of this costs money and takes a great deal of time and effort.

Visualization, on the other hand, costs nothing more than a little mental effort on your part. It can be done anywhere, even on the most restricted ranges, and can even be done when you don't have a gun available. It is, I believe, one of the least talked-about yet immensely valuable tools available in defensive training of all types.

Allowing your mind to construct the circumstances of a defensive gun encounter gives you the context that's missing from otherwise static range training. Your mind can replace the things that are missing, the things that aren't there on the range but will be there when you're attacked. It also allows you to experience an event that hasn't happened (and, hopefully, will never happen): being forced, because of an immediate threat on your life or the life of a loved one, to use your firearm to stop an attacker.

I've found that visualization is most useful in drills that simulate a full defensive shooting response: recognition of a threat, reaction to that threat, draw-

Visualization of an attacker can help bring reality into your training.

ing the gun, firing a non-predetermined number of rounds, a 360-degree search for additional threats, reluctant reholstering of the gun. It's best used to supply missing parts of the defensive response: the attacker and the conditions under which you're attacked. A skill-building drill, where you're working on a specific physical task or manipulation, isn't an appropriate venue for visualization because it's not in the context of responding to a threat.

(This isn't to say that you can't use visualization techniques as a part of your skill building, in the way that archers or golfers might, to fix in your mind the correct technique. As many athletes have shown, it can have benefits; that's a little beyond the scope of this book, however. I encourage you to explore the topic on your own, as you might find it useful.)

It's important that you do not use photo-realistic targets for visualization. The visual image tends to over-ride your imaginary image, which defeats the purpose of the technique. Instead use a quasi-humanoid form, like a body-shaped silhouette. As any good cartoonist can tell you, a face without specific features can be anyone in your mind, but the more features and shading are added the more like a specific person the drawing becomes. The more you practice against a specific person, the more likely you are to fix in your mind a view of what an attacker will always look like — which might slow your response if the real attacker you face looks nothing like what you expect.

## USES OF VISUALIZATION TECHNIQUES

Start your visualization practice by first using it to simply replace the missing attacker. As you face your target allow your mind to see not the paper or cardboard, but a living attacker showing both a weapon and some sort of intent: a raised knife, a gun being leveled in your direction, etc. Visualize to whatever level of detail you can the attacker's attributes like height, weight, sex, ethnicity, clothing, facial hair, glasses, hats, hairstyles, eye color, missing teeth, shoes, belt, coat, and anything else you think relevant.

You'll find that your first attempts are relatively crude, but as you get used to using the technique you'll be able to become more and more specific.

One caution must be made, and it's related to the admonition about photo-realistic targets: don't allow yourself the false belief that all attackers fit some specific profile. Vary what you see in your mind; throw in a woman occasionally. (Females can be attackers too, and in fact are often better at it than men because we're socially conditioned not to think of them as criminals. Visualization can help you overcome that dangerous bit of reverse sexism!) For the same reason, don't assume that only specific ethnic groups are involved in vicious attacks; it may very well be the clean-shaven white guy who looks like he just stepped out of an accounting office that comes at you with the switchblade, not the dark skinned young man who your preconceptions might have lead you to suspect as an assailant. Again, social conditioning might work to your disadvantage if you assume that all criminals look like they just came from Central Casting. Change your attacker every time you run a drill, and try to never use the same person twice.

As you engage the target, allow yourself to see the threat giving up (perhaps by dropping his weapon and throwing his hands up) to give yourself the indication that you need to stop shooting. This should be after an unplanned number of rounds have been fired;

**Not everyone fits the 'thug' profile - It's important that you not allow yourself to stereotype your attacker during visualization.**

A scenario visualization, putting you into the action in a familiar surrounding, will help you with the application of your skills.

somewhere between one and five is a good range. When you "see" the threat draw your gun (or retrieve it from its storage place) and fire until the threat has ceased. Don't preplan your shots, but allow yourself to imagine the threat stopping.

As you get better at this you can add in some movement, facial expressions, and even dialogue to better replicate a real attack scenario. Allow your mind to make the visualization as real as you can.

Once you've had some experience with static visualizations you can progress to visualized scenarios. Imagine yourself walking out of a building and through a parking lot, where you suddenly encounter your attacker and are forced to respond with lethal force. (Remember that lethal force isn't warranted just because you're annoyed or concerned; your use of force must be appropriate legally and ethically. If you're at all unclear on those concepts, I suggest seeking out the books and classes given by Massad Ayoob or Andrew Branca. Visualizing an inappropriate use of force isn't what we're after!) Imagine pre-assault cues or the kind of distraction and flanking maneuvers criminals commonly use when setting up an attack. (Again, if you're not familiar with these things it's in your best interest to educate yourself.)

Imagine, for instance, the attacker coming around the back of your car, or between parked cars, or perhaps from behind the bushes on the side of your house. Whatever the scenario, imagine your behavior and movements just before you became aware of the threat. Just like the advice to vary the threat him/

self, vary your imagined environment: your house, your neighborhood, your bedroom, the office, your favorite restaurant, the place you bank, the coffee shop you stop at every morning, the park where you walk your dog, the local movie theater, inside the shopping mall, and any other environment in which you're likely to find yourself in your normal course of activities. I'm sure you can come up with far more examples from your own life, and the more you do the greater the number of practice sessions you can have.

When you've gotten used to visualizing the threat and the conditions under which you're forced to use your firearm, add in the aftermath. With the threat neutralized, look around and visualize the scene. If it's a parking lot, for instance, look around and see the other cars, the light poles, the building from which you just came, the onlookers who are still processing what they just witnessed, and perhaps even accomplices of the attacker (there is a drill later in this book which makes use of that specific visualization).

As you can see, there is an almost unlimited number of scenarios you can create in your mind's eye. Again, don't get into a rut by visualizing the same thing again and again; be sure to mix up the environment and the attacker to give you more realistic opportunities. Also be sure to visualize a true threat — the loudmouth in the restaurant calling you names isn't the time to be drawing your gun, so it's not the time to visualize your need to do so. Visualize an articulable threat to your life or to the lives of the innocents around you and react only to that.

# CHAPTER FOUR

# TARGETS FOR DEFENSIVE SHOOTING PRACTICE

**E**very defensive shooting instructor, it seems, has his or her pet target — the one he or she believes to be absolutely necessary to "good" defensive shooting training.

I am not one of those people. I think that good defensive practice isn't dependent on a single target, and I use many targets because each allows me to teach or train something important. I'll use one for a specific aspect of the training, and for a different skill or concept I might use a completely different target because it makes teaching something else easier.

Just because a target gets used in a class doesn't necessarily mean that it's the best one for the job (or the only one for the job). Sometimes in a class setting I'll pick a target because it's educationally efficient; it allows me to teach several different lessons without needing to change targets after every string of fire. In a large class, the time saved can be substantial. By yourself, that target may not be as useful or productive.

I'm generally not a big fan of the photo-realistic targets that are available. They are relatively limited in number, and I believe their realism to be counterproductive. If you're constantly using the same half-dozen images to represent bad guys, I think it's plausible to condition yourself to believe that attackers can only look like them. Do I think that a real attacker who doesn't look like that will paralyze you into inaction? No, that would be silly; but I do think that it will cause you to take more time to identify the real threat and interfere with your recognition and decision-making. As I previously pointed out, female criminals have certainly used societal conditioning to their advantage, and it's not inconceivable that it could work the same way in reverse.

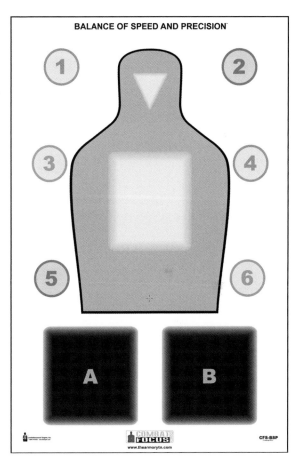

LE Targets # CFS-BSP

Here are some of the targets I use and some reasons why I use them. All are available from Law Enforcement Targets, a long-standing supplier of targets for sport and training (www.letargets.com).

Two of my favorite targets are the SEB targets

(SKU: SEB) and the Combat Focus® target (CFS-BSP). Between the two, I definitely prefer the latter, as it gives me more options, but either is a good, all-around target design. They have areas of differing precision, colors and/or numbers for randomized target calls, and their high center chest positioning of the primary shooting area is acceptable (though some might argue an oval more closely represents the actual zone of most rapid incapacitation). If I were allowed to use only one target, it would be the CFS-BSP.

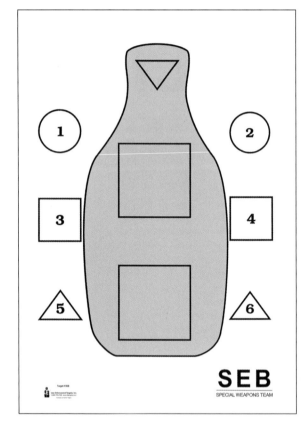

**LE Targets # SEB**

I use LE Target's Discretionary Command Training Target (SKU: DT-2A, DT-2B, DT-2C) for some drills. This is rightly thought of as a target set, as the same target comes in three variations with different combinations of numbers, colors, and shapes on each target. I find this combination, properly employed, to be invaluable in teaching target identification in chaotic environments — in other words, forcing the student to figure out if they have an actual threat before resorting to lethal force.

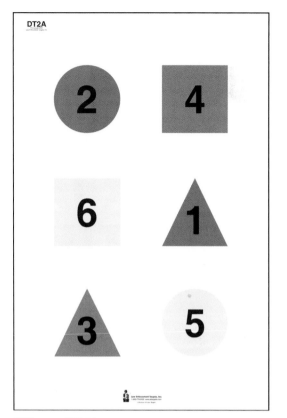

**LE Targets #DT-2A**

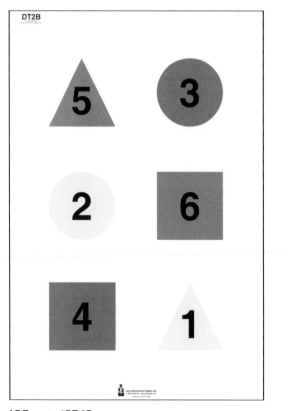

**LE Targets #DT-2B**

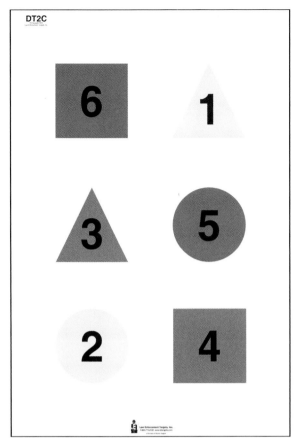

**LE Targets #DT-2C**

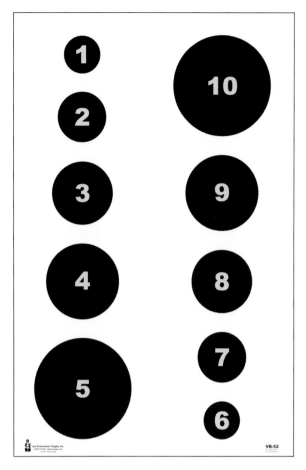

**LE Targets #VB-52**

In recent years I've become a fan of their Military Varied circle Command Training Target (SKU: VB-52), which allows me to practice varying degrees of precision on the same target. Combined with a partner calling out random numbers and perhaps some changing distances (and maybe a math problem here or there just to make sure the shooter is thinking), it makes for a good way to internalize the concept of the balance of speed and precision. It is surprisingly flexible and useful. (I usually refer to this as the "polka-dot target.")

All of the targets I've mentioned require 24-inch-wide target frames. Unfortunately many ranges, particularly those catering to competitive shooting (such as USPSA/IDPA), use a narrower 18-inch target frame. This severely limits the targets you can use, but the Colored Command Target of KR Training (SKU: KRT-1) is a good alternative for the narrower frames. Despite its compact dimensions, it has a lot of options and is therefore one of the most versatile choices you can make. I would not feel hamstrung if the situation forced me to rely on this target, and if you have narrow target frames you can easily use it in place of the #CFS-BSP.

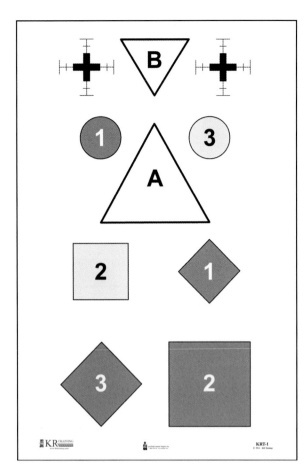

**LE Targets #KRT-1**

## DO YOU NEED TO BUY TARGETS?

Most definitely not! If you understand the specific drill and the reasons behind it you can make your own targets quite reasonably. If you have some blank paper and spray paint (or wide-tipped felt markers) you can make all of the targets you'll ever need, on demand. (One of my recent students told me he uses butcher paper and a sign-making marker, which is a one-inch-wide felt brush that you dip into a can of brightly colored water-based ink. They're used to make all kinds of signs, from those used in grocery store windows to banners for homecoming parades. I'm told they're quite economical, too.)

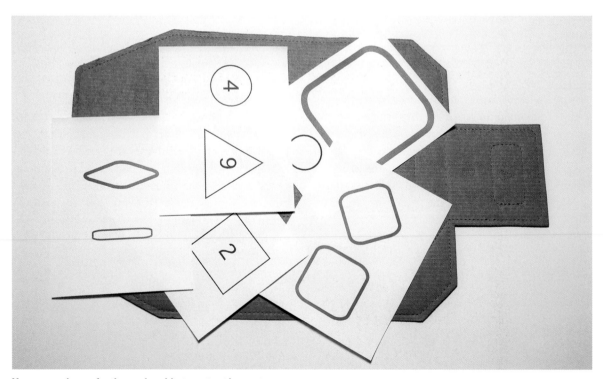

**You can make perfectly serviceable targets at home, too.**

It's not who made the target, or how it was made; it's how the target is used that's important. If you read the drill descriptions, and think about the intent of the drill, making a target is the easy part.

Don't let yourself be deluded into believing that there's some special target that will make you a better defensive shooter, because there isn't. Don't obsess over not having the 'right' target; make something that will do the job and then fill it full of holes!

I've also designed some targets that you can download (in PDF format) and print for free from my site, www.grantcunningham.com/freetargets.

## A WORD OF CAUTION ON TARGET DESIGN

As I've said, these aren't the only targets you can use. I use them, however, because of their utility, flexibility, and applicability to defensive training. You may find that you prefer to use a different target (perhaps even one that you've designed yourself), and that's perfectly fine as long as you pay attention to a few important details:

- Don't use any target that has multiple overlaid scoring areas, like the common bulls-eye, regardless of shape. One of the key things you need to train yourself to do is to recognize the level of precision that you need to achieve, and having more than one level of precision for any given target point derails that process. If you have more than one possible area for a "hit," it's too easy to allow yourself to excuse your misses: "I really meant to hit the 'B' zone"; "it would still stop him!"; "it's an 85% score." You need a target that gives you a yes/no decision: either you hit within the level of precision the target required, or you didn't. It's perfectly fine to have many targets on one sheet that have varying levels of precision, as long as they're separate from each other. (If you're unsure about this concept, please refer to my earlier books "Defensive Revolver Fundamentals" or "Defensive Pistol Fundamentals" for a complete discussion about precision and accuracy.)

- When choosing a humanoid form target, make sure that the primary area of precision is in the high center chest. The old B-27 silhouette target, for instance, has overlaid scoring areas (which are bad enough) located at 'center mass' — an area located (approximately) below the sternum. That was fine for the days when we didn't understand a whole lot about what it takes to stop a human attacker, but over the years we've learned that the fastest route to incapacitation is to do damage to the heart and large blood vessels found in the upper chest. Don't allow yourself to be trained into thinking that the abdomen is a proper aim point just because some 70-year-old target says so.

- If you're making targets by hand, don't obsess over perfection. You don't need perfect circles or perfect rectangles. I've had more than one student complain when I've spray-painted additional areas on their target sheet and my poor excuse for circles didn't exactly match those of the target next to them. This isn't a competition where you're trying to make everything even and fair; what you're trying to do is to learn and practice your ability to deliver rounds to whatever level of precision the target requires. If that's into an irregular shape, it's just a different challenge. If they're of a slightly different size or shape than they were yesterday, that's fine too!

## THE LAW ENFORCEMENT TARGETS DT-2 COMBINATIONS

I mentioned the DT-2 series of targets, and these are interesting because each target version (A, B, and C) has a slightly different combinations of numbers (1 through 6); shapes (square, circle, and triangle); and color (red, yellow, and blue.) Each number, shape and color appears on each target, but not all combinations do.

As you'll see in some of the drills, I've exploited this aspect of the targets to be able to introduce an aspect of randomness into training. This reflects the reality that you don't know ahead of time what you're going to need to shoot, or even if you actually need to.

For your convenience, I've compiled a list of the possible combinations for each target. These will be used by your training partner (in those drills that utilize these targets) to keep you from knowing what you're going to shoot until the instant you're presented with the command.

## All targets have:

- Blue triangle
- Red circle
- Blue square
- Yellow circle
- 2 circle
- 1 triangle
- 4 square
- 6 square

## No targets have:

- Blue circle
- Blue 2
- Yellow 4
- Square 2
- Triangle 2
- Circle 4
- Triangle 4
- Circle 6
- Triangle 6
- Square 1
- Circle 1
- Square 1
- Square 3
- Square 5

## A & B have, but C does not have:

- Nothing!

## A & C have, but B does not have:

- 3 triangle
- 5 circle
- Blue 3
- Blue 4

## B & C have, but A does not have:

- Red square
- Yellow triangle
- Yellow 1
- Yellow 2

## Only A has; B & C do not have:

- Yellow square
- Red triangle

## Only B has; A & C do not have:

- Circle 3
- Triangle 5

## Only C has; A & B do not have:

- Red 5
- Red 6

## NOTES

_____

_____

_____

_____

_____

_____

_____

# CHAPTER FIVE

# HOW TO PICK THE RIGHT RANGE FOR YOUR PRACTICE

Sadly, there just aren't a lot of ranges that are conducive to good defensive shooting practice. If you have one nearby, you're in luck — and also in the minority.

An ideal range would allow you:

- free movement relative to the target;

- to set up targets in at least a 270-degree spread;

- to shoot those targets on angles;

- to draw from your holster;

- to fire as many shots as you deemed necessary;

- to fire those shots at the fastest speed you could muster while still getting the hits;

- to look behind you while safely holding a loaded gun; and

- to shoot past dusk, or to turn off the lights to simulate low light conditions.

As I said, that describes precious few shooting ranges. Most ranges restrict your activities in some way: don't allow you to use "humanoid" targets; require you to set up targets in front of one specific berm; require you to always be at right angles to the targets, never shooting 'cross lane'; don't allow drawing from a holster; restrict the number of rounds per string; specify a specific shooting speed; don't allow you to do anything other than look downrange when holding a firearm; and don't allow shooting past a certain time or with the lights turned low. Indoor ranges are the most likely to have these kinds of limitations.

The ideal training range doesn't need to be big, but it should be open and free of non-realistic restrictions.

Most indoor range facilities need strict rules to handle shooters of all abilities, but many also have programs where you can practice defensive skills more realistically. Ask if your range has such a program. (Photo: Black Wing Shooting Center)

The reason for these kinds of restrictions comes down to either liability concerns or shooting prejudice. The liability part is somewhat understandable: the range can't verify the training level of everyone present, and since most shooters are, in fact, untrained (or under-trained), they enact and enforce strict range rules to prevent accidents. While I don't like those kinds of places, I do understand their concerns.

It's the ranges with shooting prejudices I dislike. What do I mean by this? Those ranges, usually run by gun clubs, restrict certain activities because they're not somehow proper or polite. I once knew a board member of a gun club who didn't want anyone to use even a vaguely human silhouette because he thought guns were to be used strictly for hunting game animals. Some don't like rapid fire because it's not done in Olympic bullseye or trap shooting. If a certain interest in the shooting community doesn't happen to be their interest, they'll use their power of regulation to prevent it from happening on their turf.

Either way, any restriction is going to affect how and what you're able to train. For those people whose only choice is an extremely restricted range (no drawing, no rapid fire, no more than a fixed number of rounds in the magazine), here are some ideas to spur further creativity on your part:

- On ranges where drawing from a holster isn't allowed, very often you can substitute getting the gun out of a case, loading it rapidly, and shooting. This can simulate a home defense scenario where you're retrieving your gun from a quick access safe.

- For those where 'rapid fire' isn't allowed (usually defined as more than one round per second), you can work on a rapid first shot response. Since these ranges usually don't allow drawing from a holster, either, start with the gun in a high ready position (gun pointed downrange, close to your body at roughly the base of the sternum, elbows tight in to your sides) and quickly extend out as you trigger a shot when you reach extension. (Read the Press Out! drill for more instruction.)

- For those that allow only a small number of rounds in a magazine, load them randomly so that you never know how many rounds you'll be able to fire before being forced to reload. This will give you practice in recognizing the need to reload.

The best solution, of course, is to find a range that will allow you to do the things you need in order to practice realistically. If that means a drive you can only make every few months, make that drive rather than handicap yourself so badly. I'm not of the opinion that 'any trigger time is good'; under severe restrictions, it may amount to little more than turning money into loud noises.

# CHAPTER SIX

# PRACTICING WITH INTEGRITY

**Managing recoil requires technique and practice - it's work!**

An interesting title for a chapter, wouldn't you say? What does it mean to practice with integrity?

It's a complicated question, actually, but one I think is important to understand if you're to get the most out of your practice time.

Practicing defensive shooting skills is work — actual work, both physically and mentally. You have to repeatedly draw your gun from your holster, conform your body into positions it's not accustomed to, make your fingers work in concert in very specific ways,

and deal with controlling the gun in your hand as it recoils from the shots. Not only that, but you have to carry a bunch of heavy gear and ammunition to and from the range when the weather may not be perfectly comfortable.

The physical work is, for some people, easier than the mental work. Shooting practice requires concentration, and lots of it, if you're to get value from the session. You may have to focus on remedial practice of the skills you're not yet good at, and at the same time not allow yourself to be distracted by any physical

**Shooting zombies with your buddy is a lot of fun, but don't kid yourself - it's not training for a real encounter.**

discomfort. Since the brain uses 20% of the body's energy (www.scientificamerican.com/article/thinking-hard-calories/), it's understandable how those levels of concentration might induce fatigue.

It's not just the thinking and concentration that induce weariness, either. If you're practicing to defend yourself from a lethal attack, you have to confront your innate fear of death. Confronting fears is distasteful, and so most people avoid doing so. If you're going to the range to practice skills to be used when you've been attacked, at some level you're confronting your fears; perhaps holding them in check while you do what's necessary to survive.

If you add all of that together, it's easy to understand the common tendency to turn a practice session into playtime, a 'fun with guns' outing instead of a time to solidify vital survival skills. Instead of getting into a solid shooting stance, the type you're likely to adopt when your fighting instincts have been activated, you might let yourself shoot in a more leisurely manner. You might allow more misses, or rationalize your inability to deliver a certain level of precision. You might pick targets that are fun (zombie targets are all the rage right now) instead of targets that you actually need to work to hit with accuracy.

Integrity as a student of defensive shooting means that you acknowledge the skills necessary to defend yourself in plausible situations and dedicate yourself to practicing those skills in context — in the manner in which they are likely to be used. It means that you work on your deficiencies instead of letting them slide, that you shoot from positions that are likely instead of those that are comfortable, and that you don't let the conditions under which you practice interfere with what you know you need to do.

Integrity means not paying lip service to practicing. It means recognizing that these skills, however uncomfortable, tiring or unsettling they may be, are likely to be critical to your surviving a brutal attack. It means that you don't substitute game play for defensive shooting, and it means that you'll do all of this as often as necessary to maintain your skills.

It also means not worrying about what the other people at the range think about what you're doing. Defensive shooting practice looks different than target shooting or plinking, and is more intense than even competition shooting. There are people who will snicker, for instance, as you practice looking around and behind before you reluctantly re-holster your gun after firing a few rounds. Integrity means that you ignore them rather than let their ignorance change your behavior.

Don't let your own insecurities, or those of others, dissuade you from doing the things you need to do to maintain your defensive skills. Practice with integrity.

# CHAPTER SEVEN

# ADDING MOVEMENT TO DRILLS

Movement at right angles to the line of attack is a useful skill to learn and practice.

When you're practicing your defensive shooting drills, you're not really practicing any particular fixed response to any particular stimulus; you're practicing skills that might be used, and if your instructor has done his or her job correctly those skills are pertinent to the widest possible range of likely incidents.

One of these skills is movement. You wouldn't think you'd need to learn (let alone practice) moving — after all, you do it all the time — but moving in the context of a defensive shooting, with a gun in your hand, is something you likely don't do every day and thus need to practice.

Whether your instructor called it 'getting off the X,' 'lateral movement,' or 'moving off-line,' the goal is the same: to make it a little harder for your attacker to mount a lethal threat against you, while simultaneously bringing your gun into action.

This is why, in the chapter on picking the right range, I specified that the ideal range would allow you to move relative to the targets — particularly in a line running perpendicular to the targets. This allows you to practice the kind of movement that is generally considered ideal: unexpected, rapid, and in a direction that makes it hardest for your opponent.

In virtually all of the drills where the gun starts in the holster, it's possible (and, I would argue, desirable) to include off-line movement as part of the drawstroke. It's not an instinctive act and thus it requires practice.

In addition to movement as part of the draw, I'd encourage you to practice movement while reloading. If your gun is out of the fight for a couple of seconds (even the best of us are likely to take that long to reload our pistols), that's a long time; certainly long enough for the bad guy to do major damage to you if you just stand in one place. During your reloads, practice moving offline and keep moving until you've got the gun reloaded.

Part of this movement can be moving to simulated cover, both as part of the draw and during a reload.

Again, this isn't a skill that is applicable in every instance. You may be constrained by environmental factors that render rapid movement to one side impractical if not impossible, but when you do have that opportunity it's best if you've practiced the move beforehand. Thus my recommendation to add movement to those drills where it's appropriate (and assuming your range allows it).

If you've had no instruction in the proper integration of this kind of movement (or of any other technique mentioned in this book), I urge you to seek out someone qualified to show you the most efficient and safe methods of doing so.

**Perhaps the best movement to practice is moving rapidly to a position of cover.**

# CHAPTER EIGHT

# THE ROLE OF THE SHOT TIMER

If you've been waiting for me to say something controversial, here it is!

At one point in my life I was an avid competition shooter. I would generally shoot three matches a month, sometimes four, most of the year. If you've never shot competition, one of the major tools used in scoring each competitor is the shot timer. I used the shot timer to measure how fast I could shoot, how quickly I could reload, and the total time it took me to complete a specified course of fire.

Because I was an avid competitor I had my own shot timer. (Several of them, actually. Shot timers, it turns out, are a little like guns themselves — I was always looking for just the 'right' one!) I used it in every practice session because my shooting heroes all said that it was the best thing to use to increase my skill level.

The defensive shooting world, populated as it was by competition shooters, tended to follow the same orthodoxy and thus to this day you'll find shot timers in the hands of most defensive instructors.

Except mine.

The shot timer, I've come to believe, is the most over-rated tool in the defensive shooter's training arsenal. I'm not saying it doesn't have its uses, mind you, only that it isn't as universally valuable as most people make it out to be.

The major problem with using a shot timer indiscriminately is that it can lead to making small concessions just to beat the timer. There are many who would say that's fine, as the faster you can do something the better off you'll be in a defensive shooting. I don't think that's logically supportable; a really good example is in reloading the revolver.

As it happens, the fastest method I found to reload a revolver (and I was a serious revolver competitor) is also the method most likely to result in a case-under-extractor jam. Wanting to get faster and faster at my reloads to beat the guys with autoloading pistols, I made changes to my technique that allowed me to substantially speed up my reloads but left me vulnerable to a case-under-extractor. However, I'd never experienced one and therefore discounted the possibility.

Long story short, in a year-end match where I had a virtual lock on a first-place finish, my super-fast reload — which had worked perfectly for me all season — caused the dreaded extractor jam at a crucial point in the match, and I ended up at the bottom of the pack.

It was just a match, a mere competition. Had that been a defensive shooting, my focus on beating the timer rather than working on more reliable and stress-resistant techniques might have resulted in a serious complication. This is the risk of relying on the shot timer as your primary arbiter of technique.

More to the topic, I teach students to always shoot as fast as they can get accurate hits at any given level of required precision. (Again, see my books "Defensive Revolver Fundamentals" and "Defensive Pistol Fundamentals" for a more thorough discussion of the relationship between accuracy and precision.) If they start missing, that likely shows they're shooting too fast; if their groups are tightly centered in the target area, they're probably shooting much too slowly. It's easy, then, to practice and train by paying attention to the target instead of the timer.

After all, if you're always shooting as fast as you can (and you should be), what does it matter how fast that is — or how fast it was yesterday? Just because you *can* measure something doesn't mean it's *important* to measure.

Now that I've told you why I'm no longer a shot timer fanatic, I'll share with you some legitimate uses I've found for the shot timer in defensive shooting practice.

First, I don't usually use the timer to measure how

**The shot timer can be a useful tool, but its application is far more limited than most believe.**

quickly I can complete a certain drill or scenario; that's a use which is dangerously ripe for the error of adjusting technique to the timer, rather than to the circumstances and conditions under which you'll actually shoot. There is an exception, however, when the drill is practicing a specific and limited skill. I do use the timer to do several things.

I've found that a reasonable mastery of a particular skill occurs when the execution of that skill becomes very consistent. During the learning phase execution is erratic, unpredictable; one repetition you might complete the movement in a certain amount of time, while the next rep takes half again (or even more) time. For instance, if I'm doing the Press-Out drill (one extension and one accurate shot) I'll use the timer to keep track of how consistently I can do it. It's a simple drill which I've been doing for years, and if for some reason I'm suddenly not doing it consistently I know that something is wrong; most likely, I've gotten lazy and am not applying full control to the process. The timer helps me pinpoint where an error might be occurring, and allows me to find the error and correct it.

Very often I'll use the shot timer to verify if I really am shooting as fast as I can get the hits. I know this sounds contradictory to what I said above, but it's not. It's very easy to start into a practice session and have some misses, then slow down to get the hits and stay in the resulting rut. That's not necessarily an indicator of ability, but can very often be a sign of

laziness. In the chapter on practicing with integrity, I mentioned that it's easy to become lazy — to not apply your skill because it requires effort. When that happens to me (and it does!) I'll slow down, get my hits, and keep shooting at that speed even though I'm capable of doing much better. The problem is, once I've got the problem corrected, I may not speed back up and shoot to my ability unless I have something to motivate me.

If that's the case I'll use the shot timer to push myself, to give myself a 'kick in the pants' by forcing me to shoot faster and still get the hits. I do this to students in class all the time (though I don't necessarily use a timer; I might clap or count at the speed I want them to shoot). Almost without exception, students find out that if they really apply their skill they can actually shoot twice as fast — or faster — as they had been!

You don't necessarily need a shot timer for this. In fact, it's sometimes more effective to use a metronome app on your smartphone to supply the required motivation. The concept, however, is the same.

I'll also combine those two concepts, using the shot timer to make sure my cadence of shots is consistent. Again, consistency is usually a good sign that the fundamentals are being well practiced, and by looking solely at the breaks between shots in a long string of fire I can see if I'm really as consistent as I think I am. (By long strings of fire, I mean a full cylinder or magazine.) To be clear, I'm not looking at sheer speed, just the consistency of my shooting.

The shot timer's random start function is helpful to make your indication of the need to shoot just a little less predictable. It's not a replacement for a training partner in any sense, but it does help break the anticipation of the shot. Most of the drills in this book can use a shot timer in this manner and you may find it very helpful to do so when you're by yourself.

The shot timer has some valuable and legitimate uses, but it's not the panacea that many people make it out to be. You can, in fact, get along quite handily without one, and I've structured the drills in this book so that they don't require a shot timer. It is, however, a good diagnostic tool when used sparingly and intelligently.

# CHAPTER NINE

# SAFETY FIRST!

Firearms are dangerous things. It's precisely because of the danger they pose that they make good tools to stop bad people from doing bad things to good people. That's why they're useful to protect you and your loved ones, but they're only useful if they're used properly.

Used improperly they present a danger to you or to innocent people. That's not what conscientious, competent, law-abiding gun owners should want to have happen, and it's why you need to approach handling your guns — including using them for training and defensive practice — with safety first and foremost.

Guns are always dangerous, but the risk you face (the chance of that danger affecting you) changes depending on what you're doing. You can change the level of risk by observing safety rules and procedures. Those rules and procedures help make sure that the benefit you get from training or practicing with your gun outweighs the risk.

For instance, shooting a pistol makes an extremely loud sound and poses a very real danger to your hearing. You reduce the chances of that happening — your risk — by wearing good hearing protection. By doing so you will reduce the risk well below the benefit you'll get from shooting that gun, whether that benefit is simply recreational or preparation for saving your life.

For any drill that you do, or any class that you take, the benefit of doing or taking has to outweigh the risk involved.

Whether you're doing any of these drills or simply handling a gun, you can reduce the risk to yourself and the people around you by following, and making sure everyone else follows, these easy-to-remember rules:

**1** Always keep the muzzle pointed in a generally safe direction whenever possible. (A generally safe direction is one where, should the gun inadvertently discharge, it will not hurt you or anyone else. This changes from environment to environment, and requires that you always think about where the safe direction happens to be.)

**2** Always keep your trigger finger outside of the triggerguard until you are actually in the act of firing. (The preferred place is straight along the frame above the trigger, which you'll often hear referred to as the "index" position. A finger that's "indexed" is in a safe position.)

**3** Always keep in mind that you are in control of a device that, if used negligently or maliciously, can injure or kill you or someone else. (This means that you must always think about what your target is, where your bullets will land, and all the other things that could result in your gun causing human suffering.)

Safety is your most important responsibility. Whenever you pick up a gun, think about what you're doing and why. Reduce your risk, and help those around you reduce theirs by teaching them these rules.

In addition to rules, ranges or specific activities may also have administrative directions or procedures to follow that augment and strengthen the basic safety rules. One of those is defining that "generally safe" direction for you. For most ranges, the generally safe direction is always downrange: pointed at the backstop or earth berm.

In this book, some of the drills require you to do a 360-degree search of your area after you've finished shooting. That's a skill you should practice after any string of fire and before you re-holster your gun. I understand that in the "real world" you may be moving around, perhaps with your muzzle depressed and pointing at the ground, as you make that search. On a range, however, that's not allowed; from an administrative standpoint you need to do your search under the artificial limit of always keeping the muzzle pointed safely at the backstop. It's a little awkward to do, but by moving your feet and turning your body you can keep the muzzle pointed downrange and still see directly behind you.

*Whenever doing a search, this administrative procedure must be followed. If you have a training partner, he/she must be informed of this requirement and asked to watch the muzzle of your gun to make sure that it stays pointed downrange at all times.*

# CHAPTER TEN

# HOW TO USE THIS BOOK

In the next section you'll find drills listed and grouped according to their goals or the conditions of the range on which you shoot:

- *Drills You Can Do By Yourself* are just that: shooting exercises that don't need a training partner to be effective or instructive.

- *Drills With A Partner* are exercises that require another person in order to complete effectively. The other person doesn't need to be a shooter, but they do need to understand how the drill works and what's required of them.

- *Basic Scenario Drills* are simple drills that bring some reality back into your training, by replicating the conditions or circumstances under which you might need to use your defensive handgun. The replications may seem a little abstract, but they're effective at helping you explore the application of your skills in better context.

## WHERE DID THESE DRILLS COME FROM?

Drills get passed around the defensive shooting world on a regular basis, and for many in this book the originator of the drill is unknown (or disputed). In other cases, it's a drill I came up with for my own needs or one which I modified from someone else's already existing drill. I've made an effort to credit the drills to the source from which I learned them, but in many cases the drills are so common that it's hard to trace their origin.

The names of the drills are generally descriptive, but there are cases where the commonly accepted name isn't terribly revealing as to the nature of the drill. There are also a few that I've either come up with on my own or modified to an extent that a new name was warranted.

You'll also find some drills that go by numerous names. The Moving Point of Aim drill, for instance, is also known variously as Wobble Zone, Dynamic Deviation Control, and The Shake Drill. In this case, I use the name by which I was introduced to the drill (by a great instructor named Georges Rahbani).

## WHY THESE SPECIFIC DRILLS?

These drills were chosen because they help to teach or reinforce very specific skills. Nothing was put here just for fun, and none of them are out of context; all of them have a definite and definable application to the specialized world of self-defense shooting.

You'll also note that none of them are generalized or nebulous. You won't see drills that are designed to improve 'gunhandling' or 'marksmanship.' Instead, every drill has a purpose — an objective, a task or skill it's specifically designed to address. Your time and money (and most likely your ammunition) are limited, and wasting any of them isn't very efficient. Every drill here has a reason for being here, and in every description you'll find that reason.

## DO YOU NEED TO USE SPECIFIC TARGETS?

For every drill I've listed the targets from the Law Enforcement Targets catalog that I've found most useful for the drill. As I mentioned in the chapter on target selection, you can make your own substitutes. As long as you pay attention to the objective of the drill, you should have no trouble coming up with a workable substitute target.

## WHY ARE THERE NO 'PAR' TIMES?

One of my operating principles in defensive shooting education is that it's important for the student to progress as far as he/she is capable. Putting in arbitrary or artificial goals (or constraints) only limits what the individual can do. Pat McNamara, the principal at TMACS Inc. Training company, points out that there are two kinds of training: outcome-based (how fast) and performance-based (how well). The outcome-based approach, he maintains, sabotages our ability to perform.

Shoot as well as you can, and strive to become better relative to yourself. What anyone else can do is irrelevant to your circumstances.

## ABOUT THE LOG PAGES

Following the drill listings you'll find some log pages that give you space to record your practice activities. If you record your practice sessions in detail, you'll find that you'll be able to more easily identify those areas that need work. Practicing only what you're already good at won't make you any better, but identifying those things that need work (and even those things that you don't like, which are usually things that need work or that you don't want to face) will.

When you fill out those log pages, be honest — particularly in the space where you should put down those things you think you could be doing better. At your next range session, look at the last log to remind yourself what you did right and where you need to pay a little more attention.

## MY PERSONAL PRACTICE REGIMEN

When I go to the range (which is, sadly, not as often as I'd like) I usually run through some specific routines that I know from experience are helpful to me.

The first thing I usually do is unload my gun and do several repetitions of the Squeeze Me drill. It's very easy, particularly if I haven't shot for a while (or I've been shooting low-recoil guns or ammunition), to forget how much hand strength I need to control a defensive gun in rapid fire. It is, in fact, one of the first competencies to deteriorate — at least for me.

After that I'll do a few repetitions of dry fire trigger manipulation, just to refresh in my mind exactly what my trigger finger is supposed to be doing. It doesn't take many reps, but I've found that doing this just before live fire is more valuable than endless dry fire at home. I call this "targeted dry fire." Dry fire is both important and useful, but the way most people recommend it be done is, I feel, wasteful. Targeted dry fire gets me the repetitions I need without ingraining

bad habits (like an inconsistent or insufficient grasp).

Once finished with these preliminaries, I load the gun and do several Press-Out drills. I'm looking to see that I'm consistently bringing the gun into my line of sight and then directly out to the target. I don't want to see the muzzle dip or 'cast' (go up then down like a flycaster would do while fishing). I start slow then increase my speed of extension very rapidly. If at any point I start to see dipping or casting, I slow down and correct the problem before going on.

My next drill is almost always a Moving Point Of Aim exercise. For me, this has been the single most valuable drill I've ever shot. I do it at almost every range session and have for a couple of decades; sometimes I'll even do it at home with an Airsoft pistol. (Some of them are precise enough to hit a coathanger wire at 10 feet, which makes them more than good enough for this drill.) I've found, though, that if I've done a lot of work with those kinds of guns that I really need that first Squeeze Me drill when I'm back at the range.

The last drill I do consistently is the Press-Out drill from the holster, which allows me to integrate the entirety of the drawstroke into a final shot. By this time I've practiced all of the things that I find suffer when I haven't practiced, and I can move on to whatever objective I've set for that range session.

Beyond those, whenever possible I prefer to run partner drills, as the concepts they embody are important in the overall scope of defensive shooting. Decisional shooting in particular is an often ignored but phenomenally important skill. Not every situation is a shooting situation, and the partner drills test my ability to discern both what I need to shoot and whether I really need to pull the trigger in the first place.

I also try to work in some Strong-Arms Tactics drills into every session, and if I have the range I'll do a Going The Distance drill as well. (I'll admit, the latter is done as much for fun as anything, and almost always on steel targets just because I like the 'clang' of the bullet hitting the steel.)

No matter what, I often finish up with another Moving Point Of Aim drill, simply because I've found it so valuable.

## HOW MANY ROUNDS?

I'm not a big believer in the need to shoot hundreds of rounds in a practice session. I've found that, for most people, fatigue dramatically reduces the value of any practice session. This is hard work, and letting

**You don't need to get carried away; your gun, holster, ear and eye protection, and 100 rounds of ammo can produce solid skill development.**

yourself tire to the point that you're not doing the drills well is self-defeating. I'd rather shoot 50 rounds on well chosen and properly executed drills, than 250 rounds on sloppy repetitions of dubious drills.

For that reason I'd suggest that a solid 50-round practice session be your goal. If you can afford (or find!) 50 more rounds, and fatigue isn't an issue, then simply increase the number of drills you run or the number of repetitions of each drill. Frankly, unless you're a regular competitor, I'd seriously suggest calling it quits at 100 rounds regardless; I don't see a benefit for most people beyond that point.

## ADVICE FOR THE TRAINING PARTNER

A big part of the training partner's job is to confuse the shooter. No, really, that's the job!

A huge missing part of defensive shooting training is the need to train a response to something that we don't know is going to happen. Let's say you're in your bank lobby, for instance — as you're filling

out the deposit slip, do you have any inkling at all that someone is going to burst through the door and order everyone to the floor? Did you know ahead of time that you were going to need to shoot someone, let alone who and where?

Most defensive shooting training is predicated on knowing beforehand that something needs to be shot, what needs to be shot, where it needs to be shot, and (almost always) how many times it needs to be shot. This doesn't reflect the reality of defensive shooting at all. The goal in training needs to be to build a link between the recognition that we need to shoot and the recall of the skills to make the shot we need to make.

In order to build that recognition-recall link, we need to reduce to the greatest degree possible any anticipation of the need to shoot (let alone what, where, and how much.) The only way to do that easily on a conventional range is to present targets randomly and force the shooter to make the decision to shoot.

This is where you, the training partner, come in!

**The training partner's job is cooperative — to help with the most important part of defensive shooting: decision making in response to a changing stimulus.**

For most of the partner drills there will be multiple options, and it's your job to give the shooter his/her command (a 'call') to start the drill — but in such a way that it's not immediately apparent exactly what (if anything) they're going to shoot. It's also important that you randomize those calls so that the shooter can't predict what you're going to do next.

For each of those drills I'll suggest the commands that you can make, but as you get more comfortable with the drill and the purpose behind it you may feel free to deviate a bit to further confuse the shooter. You get to play with his/her mind in the truest sense: throwing the shooter off mental balance into a state where decisions have to be made, instead of rigid and predictable responses activated.

The first few times you do this you may find that a previously calm, collected, high-performing shooter suddenly can't hit the broad side of a barn — from the inside! I've seen it happen with highly trained SWAT team officers, and I've seen it happen with accountants. Once you push them out of their comfort zone, they fail. That's part of the learning

process and the very reason I highly recommend partner drills.

I said before that the training partner doesn't even need to be a shooter, and I hope you now understand why. You don't need to be able to shoot; you just need to be able to think a few steps ahead of your shooter and have the willingness to be a little devious!

## NOTES

_____

_____

_____

_____

_____

_____

_____

# CHAPTER ELEVEN

# DRILLS YOU CAN DO BY YOURSELF

## DRILL NAME: SQUEEZE ME

### Purpose

Your ability to control your gun during rapid fire is directly related to how firmly you're able to grasp (squeeze) it. Most people grasp the gun far less firmly in practice than they actually can, and far less than they're likely to do when they're really faced with a lethal threat and their natural alarm reactions have kicked in. Practicing at a more realistic grasp pressure helps you discover just how quickly you can fire and still get hits on target under realistic conditions. This drill helps do that by first establishing what your maximum grasp pressure is, and then establishing a mental 'picture' of the amount of hand pressure you should apply whenever you're shooting. Over time, this should result in greater hand strength as well.

Your goal should always be to get to a firing position with the optimal grasp pressure, whether you're practicing, plinking, or dry-firing. Whenever you're manipulating the trigger, for any reason and on any gun, you should be using your optimal grasp pressure.

Grasp strength is a foundational skill, but one that surprisingly few people pay attention to.

## Rounds needed

This is a non-shooting drill and can be done at home or at the range — though it's best to immediately follow up with a live fire exercise if you can. That immediate feedback on the increased control that results from an optimum grasp pressure is key to cementing in your mind the value and importance of this drill.

## Target

None needed, but I strongly suggest a bullet-resistant backstop.

## Special equipment

You should always keep the gun pointed in a generally safe direction, and for "dry practice" like this I strongly recommend that you use a safe backstop (if you're at home, a bookcase loaded with books will do, as will a basement wall).

## Description

Get a good two-handed firing grasp on the gun and extend out into your normal shooting position. Once there, start increasing the amount of pressure (squeeze) your hands exert on the gun; squeeze harder and harder, until your muscles start trembling from the effort. You should see the entire gun shake as your muscles tremble! Now relax your hand pressure just enough to stop the tremors — no more, just enough to stop the gun from shaking. That is your optimum grasp pressure.

Relax and bring the gun back to your chest, barrel parallel to the floor or ground, with your elbows at your side (this is called, variously, the "chest ready" or "high compressed ready" position - though it may have other names as well). Rest for a few seconds, then repeat the drill. Extend out to a shooting position, increase your grasp pressure until you see trembling, then back off just enough to stop the shaking. Bring the gun back to your chest and relax.

Unless you've done this sort of drill before, you probably noticed in both cases that the grasp pressure you ended up with — the pressure you're capable of exerting and still maintain complete and solid control of the gun — is far greater than what you usually use when you're shooting. It's important to memorize what that amount of pressure feels like so that you can recreate it every time you extend the gun to shoot.

To do that, repeat the drill. This time, when you back off to your optimum pressure, stop and hold it for just a few seconds and actively memorize that feel-

ing. Come back to the ready position, relax, and then do that again: extend, squeeze, tremble, back off, think and memorize that pressure level, then come back to ready and relax.

Now it's time to put that into action. As you extend out into your shooting position, go immediately to that memorized pressure level. If the gun is shaking, it means you went too far and need to back off just a bit. Repeat: extend out and by the time you reach your shooting position you should be at that memorized grasp pressure, the one that's ideal for you.

## Scoring/evaluation

This is entirely subjective. Is the pressure level you end up with much greater than you're used to grasping the gun? Can you recreate the pressure level instantly when you draw the gun or extend to shoot? Is your hand pressure increasing over time because of this exercise? Most importantly, are you remembering that pressure level and using it every time you shoot your gun?

## Variations

Try the same drill strong-hand and weak-hand only. It's even more vital to have complete control of the gun when you're shooting one-handed, and I find that this drill pays particular dividends in that department.

## Special notes

If doing this outside of a shooting range, treat it like a dry fire drill: check that your gun is unloaded, then check again. I suggest leaving the ammunition in a separate room.

## NOTES

_____

_____

_____

_____

_____

_____

_____

_____

## DRILL NAME: PRESS-OUT

### Purpose

I've come to believe that the first shot you decide to take is your best opportunity to affect your attacker's ability to hurt you. Notice that I didn't say it's the most important shot — only that it's your *best chance* to cause your attacker to stop doing harm to you.

Why might that be? As respected defensive trainers like Claude Werner and the late, great Paul Gomez have pointed out, after the first shot everything changes. People stop thinking, they start moving, bystanders start screaming, and it becomes harder to solidly land the second, third, fourth, and subsequent shots. Not impossible, mind you — folks do it all the time and shooting multiple rounds is a skill that needs to be practiced as well — but it is more difficult because of all the other "stuff" going on in the environment.

That's why, after that first round, it's going to be more difficult to get your shots into that relatively small vital area where you have the greatest likelihood of incapacitating the attacker. If the first round doesn't give good effect, it's going to mean that you'll be making the rest of your shots under more difficult circumstances and that it's going to take longer to get to your goal of ending the attack. Making the most of that fleeting opportunity is likely to improve the odds of a favorable outcome.

It makes sense, then, to spend time making sure that you can land that first shot very quickly and to whatever degree of precision the target demands. By developing a consistent, clean extension to your firing position you'll be able to more consistently deliver that first round on target. This drill helps you do that by working on the muscle control necessary to get the gun into position without deviation from your point of aim.

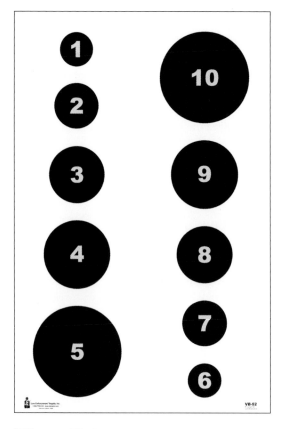

LE Targets #VB-52

This 'high compressed' or 'chest ready' position makes for efficient shooting, good retention.

This is a seemingly simple drill, but it's not! It's a drill I use myself frequently because it's an easy skill to ignore and one which seems to deteriorate easily. Frankly, I've found that the more experienced the student, the less able they are to do this drill well. Why? I'm not sure, but I think it's because this is seen as a "beginner's" exercise and thus skipped in an effort to get to the "advanced" material. Don't do that, because — as I've said — that first round is your best opportunity to get to the end of the attack!

## Rounds needed

As you're learning the skill, take as many rounds as you need to cement the concepts in your mind. However, this is a surprisingly fatiguing drill; I suggest limiting yourself to 10 or 20 repetitions at any time. When I use it as a precursor to my regular practice, I'll generally do 5 to 10 repetitions max.

## Target

You can use any target for this drill, though I prefer to use the LE Targets #VB-52 for the ability to practice this to varying degrees of precision.

## Special equipment

None.

## Setup

You'll need one target stand or hanger. Stand facing the target, starting somewhere around 3-5 yards. You can increase the distance as you build skill, but I generally recommend keeping it within likely self-defense distances — perhaps 10 or 12 yards, maximum.

## Description

Start with the gun in what's variously called a 'high ready,' 'chest ready,' or 'compressed ready' position: the gun roughly at the base of your sternum and close in to the chest, muzzle pointing downrange and parallel to the ground, with the elbows tucked in.

Pick a point on the target and focus on it. Bring the gun forward and up, into your line of sight, then directly to the target. The last 1/3, at a minimum, of your extension should be straight in line with your vision.

This is actually easier to say than to do. Most people will, as the gun starts to move upward into their line of sight, point the muzzle up and get a "flycasting" effect as the muzzle is then brought down to point at the target, as shown in this series of four images:

Some people will start with the muzzle slightly low and take something like a bowler's swing, bringing the muzzle up only as they arrive on target, as shown in this series of four images:

Both of these are counter-productive to the goal of getting to that first accurate shot as quickly as possible; they're wasted energy that leaves you unable to know when you can shoot because the muzzle doesn't actually get on target until you reach extension. What you want (and need) to do is to bring the gun into your line of sight as though it was on an escalator. That's the effect you're striving for: the gun stays level in relation to the threat as it comes up into your line of sight, then straight out to extension, as shown in this series of three images:

As you see the gun come into your line of sight, take the safety (if your gun has one) off. As you come close to the limit of your extension, your trigger finger should just touch the trigger, and at the point you reach the limit of your extension you press the trigger smoothly and quickly to fire a single shot.

The key is to have the gun aligned on target for that last 1/3 or so of travel to extension; at any point along that path you should be able to trigger a shot and end up fairly close to your aim point. The goal is to be able to trigger an accurate shot immediately on reaching extension, without having to re-aim the gun.

Take your finger off of the trigger, back into index on the frame, and bring the gun back into the high ready position. You're ready to do another repetition.

## Things to look for

Watch your gun relative to the target, and if you find yourself "bowling" or "flycasting" slow down and pay closer attention to the extension. I like to think of the escalator analogy and watch for the gun to come up into my line of sight already indexed on the target. The effect when you do this properly is, as much as I hate imprecise terms, almost magical as the gun comes into your line of sight and seemingly aligns itself on target.

## Scoring/evaluation

Your goal is a 100% hit rate. If you're missing even occasionally, check that you're at full extension (no longer moving forward) before you trigger the shot. (This is the most common cause of misses in the students I've seen.) Make sure that your grasp on the gun is at your optimum (refer back to the Squeeze Me drill) before you hit extension — you should be at optimum grasp while the gun is still extending. If you're still missing, adjust your speed of extension and timing of the shot until you can make the hit every time, and only then work to make the entire process faster.

## Variations

If you're using the VB-52 target, when you can get rapid (immediate) hits on the largest target every time, move to the next smaller target and so on as your skill increases.

You can do the same drill as part of a complete response: drawing from the holster and extending out to the target in one smooth motion. This drill can also be done dry fire, though the benefit of being able to judge the impact of the round is obviously eliminated. This can also be done with Airsoft, assuming you have an Airsoft gun that mimics your actual weapon in terms of size and shape, and taht shoots to point-of-aim.

**NOTES**

# DRILL NAME:
## MOVING POINT OF AIM

### Designer

Unknown, though I learned it from an instructor named Georges Rahbani.

### Purpose

No one, not even Olympic shooters, holds a gun perfectly still. Your gun is always moving, and the difference between an Olympian and you is that their gun just moves a lot less! Understanding and controlling that movement is the key to shooting smaller or more distant targets, or even precisely controlling hits when you're forced to shoot around innocents (which is often the case in home invasion scenarios).

While most defensive shooting incidents don't require great precision shooting skills, there is the definite minority that do. Being able to shoot to whatever plausible level of precision you might need is therefore an important skill to develop. This drill, more than any other I've used, has given me that skill and the confidence that comes from knowing how to shoot to any level of precision I might not have practiced.

This drill works partly because the source of many misses is when a shooter tries to hold the gun steady on a point on the target and 'grab' the shot before the gun moves off target. As the target gets smaller, the problem gets worse; if you're consistently shooting low on higher-precision targets, for example, you may be a victim of grabbing.

This drill helps your ability to deliver precision shots by allowing you to come to terms with the gun's movement, learn how to control it, and how to deliver precision shots by using that movement to your advantage.

### Rounds needed

The value of the drill diminishes with fatigue; it takes both physical ability and concentration. I'll usually shoot no more than 10 rounds on this drill, using the smallest circle, during a practice session.

### Target

I like to use the LE Targets #VB-52 for this drill. Start at the largest circle, and with each repetition move to the next smaller circle.

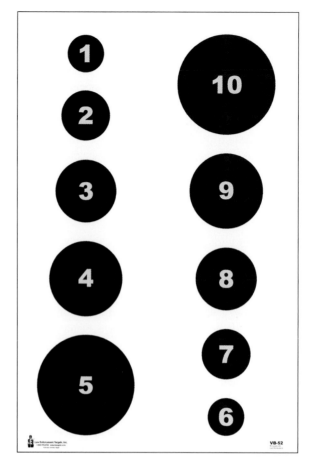

**LE Targets #VB-52**

### Special equipment

None.

### Description

**Stage 1:** Start with your gun loaded and in the ready position. Extend the gun to the largest circle and intentionally move the gun all over inside of the target area; stay inside the circle's boundaries, but deliberately move the gun (preferably in a random pattern) all over inside the circle. At random intervals, press the trigger smoothly and fire one shot without stopping the movement of the gun. As long as the gun stays inside the target area, your rounds will hit accurately no matter when you trigger the shot (or if the gun is moving when you do). This helps you internalize the idea of shooting while the gun is moving, and for a lot of people this is the hardest part of the drill. If you kept the gun from moving outside of the target boundaries, you should have all your shots inside the target area. Shoot 3-4 rounds, maximum; at this level it's pretty easy and the idea is to acquaint you with the concept.

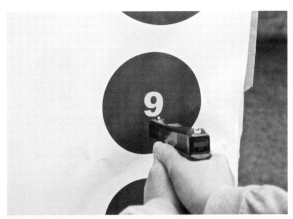

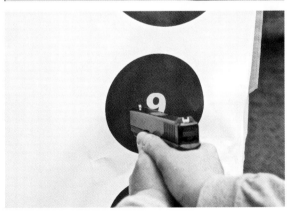

**If the gun were fired at any of these points (above four images), the bullet would hit inside the target area.**

**Stage 2:** If all of your shots landed inside the largest circle, move to the next smaller and repeat the drill. You'll still be moving the gun intentionally, but this time the target area is smaller. Your movements must of course be smaller to keep the sights inside of the circle. Just like with the larger target, as long as your sights were in the circle at all times it doesn't matter when the shot breaks, and you should have all your shots in the circle. Again, 3-4 rounds should be sufficient.

**Stage 3:** Again, if all your shots were in the last circle move to the next smaller. As the circles get smaller you'll need to concentrate only on moving the gun (sights) in the circle; as you're concentrating on the movement of the gun, simply apply continuously increasing pressure on the trigger until the gun fires. If you do this correctly, you'll be so intent on keeping the sights inside of the target area that you'll be a little surprised at the shot. Again, as long as you did the job of concentrating on keeping the gun inside the circle you should have no misses.

**Stage 4:** : Again, move to the next smallest circle and repeat. This should be getting a little harder, but if you concentrate on the fundamentals of keeping the gun moving inside the circle and concentrating on that movement as you apply pressure to the trigger, you should be rewarded with all your shots inside the target area.

**Stage 5:** : This is on the smallest circle, and this time you're not going to deliberately move the sights inside the circle. Instead, when you extend into your shooting position just allow the gun to move naturally, applying only the control you need to keep the sights in the circle. Again, you're not intentionally moving the gun this time but you are controlling the gun's movement (the "wobble") so that the sights don't wander outside of the circle. Again, concentrate on watching the sight movement and controlling it as you apply pressure to the trigger until the gun fires.

By the time you've finished Stage 5, you should have no problem putting all your rounds into the smallest circle.

## Scoring/evaluation

Pass/fail: all shots must be hits inside the area of the target on which you're aiming. The great thing about this drill is that there are really only three possible reasons for a miss (assuming you understand what a sight picture looks like, of course). Either you deliberately (if unconsciously) stopped the gun to "grab" the shot; you didn't concentrate on keeping the gun aligned inside the target area at all times; or you didn't press the trigger smoothly. Fix whichever problem it is and try again.

(I've found that the fix for a bad trigger press is to concentrate on the sight movement to the exclusion of all else; this keeps you from over-thinking the trigger press and almost always fixes the problem.)

## Variations

Combine this with a Press-Out Drill, allowing yourself the shortest "wobble time" before pressing the trigger. There is also a partner version of this drill in that section.

## Special notes

I've found this drill to be very helpful with shooters who have flinching issues, as it forces them to focus on something other than the gun going off. This drill is imperative to master before proceeding to drills at either longer ranges or those demanding greater precision, all of which utilize the lessons learned here. I consider this a foundational drill and almost always include it in my own practice sessions.

## NOTES

_____

_____

_____

_____

_____

_____

_____

_____

_____

_____

_____

_____

## DRILL NAME: EMERGENCY RELOAD

## Purpose

Reloading is actually not a commonly needed skill in self defense. In fact, outside of police service it's rare (darned near impossible, in fact) to find a defensive shooting where a reload made any difference in the outcome of the incident. Even so, it's at least plausible that you could run out of ammunition (particularly with low-capacity guns and the increasing tendency to multi-attacker crimes) and you should be able to efficiently reload in the worst-case scenario.

The interesting thing about the emergency reload is that it's not the mechanics of the procedure that are the problem. The real issue, and one which I see again and again with students, is that their reaction to needing to reload when it comes as a surprise to them is delayed. There's a span of time where they look at the gun or try to press the trigger because they haven't yet recognized that their gun is empty! The major thing that needs practice, in my opinion, is the rapid recog-

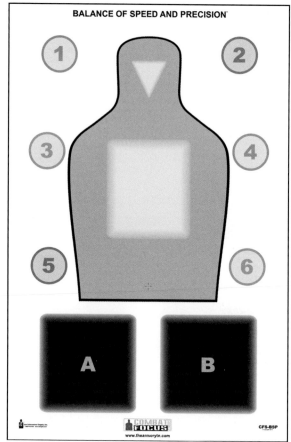

#CFS-BSP

nition of the need to reload — not the reload itself.

That's what this drill is really all about: learning to recognize the need to reload, because that's where most of your time is actually going to be taken. It also isn't so much a standalone drill as a *procedure* to be used with all other drills to reduce your ability to plan your reloads. I'm introducing it here as a separate drill so that you can see the procedure and why it's important. Doing it as a drill by itself once or twice also has the benefit of acquainting you with what a slide-lock empty condition feels like so that you learn to associate that stimulus with the physical act of reloading.

## Rounds needed

I'd suggest at least 50 for the initial drill (only if you have no real experience with doing reloads as a response to an empty gun.)

## Target

Any. I usually revert to my favorite all-purpose target, the #CFS-BSP.

## Special equipment

At least three magazines; the more you have, the better.

## Setup

Load each magazine with a different, and unplanned, number of rounds. I usually tell my students to load between 30% and 50% of the magazine's capacity.

Once you've done that, shuffle the magazines so that you don't know which is which, then stick them all into a large pocket on your weak-hand side. Once you've done that pull one out at random, put it in your normal magazine carrier, and pick another with which you'll load the gun.

## Description

On whatever start signal you prefer, shoot 2-3 rounds at the upper-chest area of the target. Concentrate on shooting quickly while getting 100% hits. Come back to the ready position (or holster the gun, as appropriate) and do it again. When you hit the point that the slide has locked back on an empty chamber, initiate your reload. The goal is to start the reload sequence *instantly* on your recognition of the slide being locked open.

## Things to look for

You should be striving to learn to recognize slidelock without having to tilt the gun back so that you can

**Load several magazines between 40% and 60% of capacity, but don't load them with the same number of rounds.**

look at the open chamber. When the gun runs empty, there's a very different feel to the recoil pattern as the slide locks open on the empty magazine (even if the magazine is empty and for some reason the slide doesn't lock back, there's still a very different feel in the gun's recoil as the slide comes forward). The gun's weight is different, and the center of gravity moves dramatically rearward. These are the indications that you're practicing to recognize.

## Scoring/evaluation

Don't let the nature of this drill lead you to be sloppy with your shots! You should be shooting as quickly as you can and still get all of your hits inside that upper chest area. If you're not, slow down and identify the problem; correct it, and speed up. If you're always concentrating on the reload you won't get the full benefit of this drill, so pay attention to getting those hits!

## Variations

During any of the other drills in this book, randomly load your magazines and mix them up. This helps with the processing overhead of trying to complete a drill instead of focusing on the reload skill itself.

## Special notes

To do this drill with a revolver, load the cylinder but leave two non-adjacent chambers empty. Before you

close the cylinder, close your eyes; spin the cylinder, stop it randomly, then close it without looking. When you hit a "click," that's your cue to reload. It's not nearly as dramatic as with an autoloader, I'll admit, but it does the trick!

## NOTES

_____

_____

_____

_____

_____

_____

_____

_____

_____

_____

**The goal of this drill is to build a recognition-recall sequence so that when the time comes you won't be staring at your gun trying to figure out what to do next.**

## DRILL NAME: THE CASCADES

### Purpose

One of the very basic defensive shooting skills is learning to recognize the amount of precision that the target requires, then applying the amount of skill necessary to place accurate shots (shots that land within the target's area of precision). The more precisely you need to shoot, the more of your skill you need to apply and the more deliberately (relatively speaking, of course) you're going to shoot. It simply takes more time to shoot to a greater degree of precision, so if the target isn't demanding it why waste the time shooting to an arbitrarily higher standard?

You won't know ahead of time what your target — your threat — is going to demand of you. Someone standing squared off in front of you presents one level of precision; standing bladed to you, another. If he's behind something the area of precision changes, and if there are innocents around the level of precision might be different. Since you don't know ahead of time what you're facing, shooting to a single level of precision all the time (no matter how quickly you can do it) doesn't prepare you for what happens when it changes. If the area of precision is larger than what you've trained for, you're likely to shoot too slowly and waste valuable time; if it's smaller, you may shoot too quickly and miss some of your shots. Understanding your own balance of speed and precision for any given target size is critical to good defensive shooting, and teaching that is the first goal of this drill.

Another basic skill is evaluating (assessing) your shooting as you shoot; are you hitting your target? If not, what do you need to change? The application is clear: when you're faced with a threat that requires shooting, you need to be able to continuously evaluate if you need to shoot another round. If not, you stop shooting; if the threat is still there, you need to shoot again. This all has to happen instantaneously, and requires the kind of practice this drill gives you; it forces you to assess as you're shooting, to gauge whether you're shooting too quickly or too slowly, missing your target or wasting time grouping rounds into a level of precision that's not needed.

This drill is designed to help you with both skills: first, to recognize a changing level of precision and control the gun to make accurate hits; second, giving you the opportunity to practice rapid assessment (evaluation) as you shoot.

### Rounds needed

You'll need approximately 25 rounds per repetition, depending on how much you miss.

### Target

This drill was built specifically around the LE Targets #VB-52; its cascading circle sizes were the inspiration for the drill name.

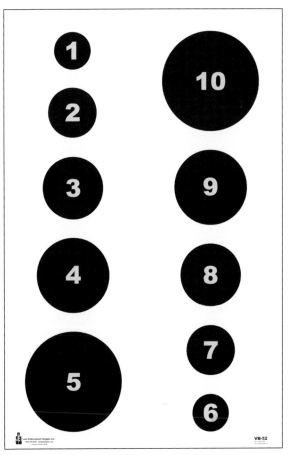

**LE Targets #VB-52**

### Special equipment

None.

### Description

Start at a comfortable and likely defensive shooting distance (around 4-5 yards). Depending on your level of training and range restrictions, you may start at a high ready (gun in front of your lower chest, elbows at your side and the muzzle pointing downrange) or with gun in the holster.

Your goal is to put 3-5 rounds into each target as quickly as you can with no misses.

Begin the drill on the largest circle; decide just be-

**Misses on the smaller target show the shooter doesn't yet have a grasp of the fundamentals or doesn't yet understand his own balance of speed and precision.**

fore you start how many shots you'll put into the circle, then shoot as fast as you can get those hits. If you miss, you need to recognize your miss, correct your technique, and fire another round to get a hit. This should happen without pulling the gun down and out of your line of sight; you need to stay in a shooting position, extended on the target. The goal is 3-5 HITS per circle, not 3-5 rounds fired at the circle!

Stop shooting and come back into the ready posi-

tion when you have the number of hits you predetermined when you started; your last shot cannot be a miss. If you decided that you were going to get 4 hits on the circle, and you hit 3 in a row and missed the fourth, you need to fire another round to get to your self-selected goal. Don't cheat yourself on this.

Once you've shot one circle, move to the next smallest and repeat the drill. If you started from the holster, re-holster and start from there again.

## Scoring/evaluation

Your goal is 100% hits. If you find yourself missing, that's an indication you need to fix something about your technique: perhaps your grasp isn't sufficient, or you're shooting before you hit your normal full extension, or maybe your trigger control is bad. If all of those things are fine, it may be that you're simply shooting faster than your current level of skill will allow on that particular target, which is your indication that you need to apply more control to the gun at that level of precision. That means you'll need to slow down to apply that level of control.

If you find all of your rounds clustering in a small group inside a circle, that's an indication you can shoot faster at that target size. Increase your shooting speed by 50% and try that target again. When you get to the point you're starting to miss occasionally, slow down just a bit — that's your current skill level (balance of speed & precision) for that target size (level of precision).

If you find yourself shooting the same speed on the smaller targets as you did on the bigger ones, that's a sign that you're not shooting at an appropriate level of precision for some of the targets. If you're shooting the small targets as fast as the larger ones but missing, you need to slow down as the target precision increases; if you're shooting the small targets at the same speed and getting your 100% hit rate, that's your clue that you can shoot the larger targets a lot faster than you have been!

Correct any obvious errors and run the drill again on the other set of circles. If you've got a good handle on your abilities — on your own balance of speed & precision — you'll notice a definite change in your shooting pace between the largest and the smallest, and you'll have all your hits inside all of the circles without clustering in the middle.

## Variations

If you're starting at the high ready, move sideways (perpendicular to the line between you and the target) at least a full body width as you extend the gun. This helps you practice evasive movement ("get off the X") as well as practicing coming to a stop and into a stable shooting position.

### Designer

From a drill by I.C.E Training

### Purpose

Controlling your gun in a realistic string of fire is an often-overlooked skill. Many people train to give two very fast shots to the target before moving to the next target, stopping to evaluate, or quitting altogether. It's easier to control a "double tap" or "hammer" (yes, I know they're technically two different kinds of shot pairs, but the consequence is the same) than it is to control three or four shots made at the same rate. I've had many students challenge me on this assumption, and I ask them to shoot the fastest double tap they can; the shots usually land very close to each other. Then I ask them to shoot five rounds at the exact same pace with the same hits, and very few are able to do so.

Why is this important?

When I see videos of actual defensive shooting incidents, regardless of the shooter's training I don't see the bangbang—bangbang—bangbang of consecutive double taps; what I see instead is bangbangbang-bangbangbang — a continuous string of shots until the threat disappears. A problem potentially occurs when a shooter, used to the higher controllability of the double tap, finds him or herself suddenly shooting that rapid string and, like most students I see, unable to control their gun in a realistic string of fire. Why do we see so many instances where a large number of rounds are fired with (often) few hits? It *might* be partially attributable to this big change in control that occurs between practicing controlled pair shooting and the realities of the criminal attack.

This drill is designed to help you develop control over a long string of fire, control that is (hopefully) equal to the control you have when shooting fewer rounds.

### Rounds needed

Two full magazines, or sufficient ammunition to load your revolver twice.

### Target

You can use anything that has two targets of roughly 6-8 inches in diameter. I usually use the two lower black squares on the LE Targets #CFS-BSP target.

Old-fashioned 'two shots and assess' procedure doesn't match the reality of defensive shooting nor allow the shooter to learn proper recoil control in realistic strings of fire.

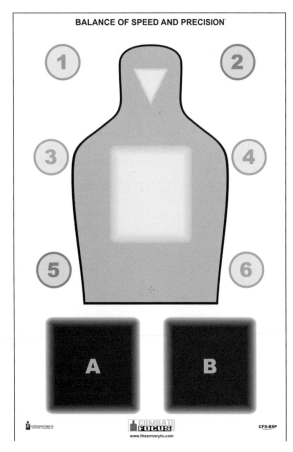

**LE Targets #CFS-BSP**

## Special equipment

Optional: This is a drill in which a shot timer can be helpful, as it allows you to check if you really are shooting as consistently as you think you are. It's not necessary, but if you have one this is one of the few legitimate uses for it in defensive shooting training.

## Description

Stand at a likely self-defense distance (around 4 yards) from the target. You'll start on the "A" box of the BSP target.

**Stage 1:** Start with the gun at full extension on one of the two identical targets, finger on trigger, and on your decision to shoot (or the command or shot timer beep) fire the gun to empty as fast as you *believe* you can get all your hits inside the target area. Your shots should be perfectly evenly timed; in other words, you should be shooting at a consistent cadence, like a metronome. If you prefer a competition analogy, you're looking for consistent split times (the time between each shot).

Reload immediately on your recognition of the empty gun. When you've reloaded, keep the gun in the chest-ready or high-compressed-ready position and take a look at the target you just shot. If you had misses, think about shooting 10-20% slower; if all of your shots were in the target with plenty of room to spare, think about what 20% faster would feel like. If you had perfect target utilization, add 10% to your speed.

**Stage 2:** You'll do everything just as you did in Stage 1, but this time make the changes to your shooting speed as outlined above. Repeat the drill at your new speed.

## Scoring/evaluation

The goal, like many of the other drills, is 100% hits on the target as quickly as you can get them. If you had any misses on the first target, set your internal clock just a little slower and re-run the drill on the second target to see if you were shooting beyond your ability at this target size and at this distance.

If your shots were closely clustered, that's an indication that you're not shooting up to your ability (your balance of speed & precision); you could shoot faster and still get hits inside the target area. That's why I had you add 20% to your time — so that you could see that your assessment of your balance was off.

If you get perfect hits, no misses but no un-needed levels of greater precision, your balance of speed & precision (your skill level) was actually good. The reason I suggested that you shoot a little faster was to get you to see what you might be able to do if you pushed yourself. If you still got all your hits at the new speed, you were probably just being sloppy or lazy the first time; if you missed one or two, it means you actually had an excellent idea of your balance on those targets.

Many times I'll watch students get ready to shoot this drill and they'll apply far more control to the gun than they do in almost any other drill in class. They know they'll be shooting a lot of rounds very quickly and that they need to control the gun, so they'll use greater grasp pressure and lean into the gun further to gain the recoil control they know ahead of time they'll need. Here's a question: how many rounds will you need to shoot when you're attacked? The only correct answer is "I don't know." If you don't know, doesn't it make sense to exert the level of control you'll need to fire a long string of rounds, since you might need to?

This is one of the major lessons in shooting this drill: If you find yourself reflexively exerting more physical control over the gun than you do when you know you're *not* going to be shooting a whole magazine, that means you're cheating your training. Regardless of the drill you're shooting, you should always exert that level of physical control over the gun, because that's what you're likely to need to do when you're really attacked.

## Variations

You can (and should) shoot this strong-hand-only for a test of your ability to control the gun when you need your other hand free. You'll notice a big change in your balance of speed & precision, and in your ability to handle the gun in long strings of fire.

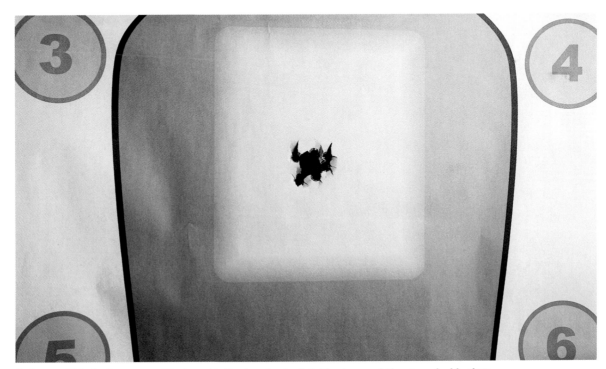

**A cluster of hits in the center of the target indicates shooter is taking too much time to make his shots.**

## DRILL NAME: CHASING PRECISION

### Purpose

One of the interesting tidbits uncovered by researcher Claude Werner, former chief instructor at the Rogers Shooting School, is that defensive shootings occasionally require a higher level of precision than we have been lead to expect. This isn't true of all cases, of course; most defensive shootings are still relatively straightforward and the physical shooting challenges usually aren't terribly great, but on occasion you do need a higher level of precision (shooting past an innocent, for instance, or where the attacker has decided to hide behind something).

This is why one of the key tenets in my courses is that you need to be able to deliver whatever level of precision the target requires. The level of precision isn't up to you; the target determines that, and your job is to recognize that level of precision and be able to deliver it on demand, without preparation.

This is as close to a purely marksmanship-driven drill as you'll find in this book. Its purpose is simply to help you develop the ability to shoot to extreme and unlikely levels of precision should you need to, and also to give you a feeling for the upper limits of your ability. It can also show you whether your gun is up to the task of delivering the precision you want it to, or that it might be called upon to deliver.

You must have a good mastery of the techniques in the Moving Point Of Aim drill in order to be able to do this well.

### Rounds needed

This is a very taxing drill from a concentration standpoint. I usually recommend shooting 6-12 rounds total, though the number is not critical, and you can learn the lesson in a very few rounds.

### Target

One sheet of white printer paper or a white paper plate.

### Special equipment

None.

### Description

Start by standing no more than three yards from the

Place one single hit in the center of the paper. That single hole is now your aiming point.

target; this is not a drill that derives any benefit from longer distances.

Get into your normal defensive shooting stance, extend on target and place one single hit in the center of the paper. That single hole is now your aiming point; stay extended on target, align your sights on that hole, and just as in the Moving Point Of Aim drill allow your sights to move within that bullet hole, but no more — concentrate on keeping the sights in that hole, allowing them to move slightly as you quickly apply continuously increasing pressure on the trigger until the gun fires. Wherever that round hit, use it as your next aiming point and repeat the drill. Do this until you run through the rounds you've allotted.

## Scoring/evaluation

Ideally, and if everything worked well, you'll have one large hole in the center of the paper! If you're exceptionally good (and your gun is properly set up) it can even look like nearly a single hole, but it's usually more akin to the size of a nickel and can often be a little egg-shaped. What you want to see are a bunch of bullet holes with no paper space between them, making one large hole; it admittedly doesn't happen very often, especially on the first try. If it doesn't look like that, the pattern of holes will tell you where your errors originated and what you need to work on.

If the holes form a fairly straight line going in any direction, this is usually an indication that your gun does not shoot to the point of aim of the sights. Sometimes it's an ammunition issue, particularly if your training ammunition is significantly different in bullet weight or velocity from your carry ammunition. If that's the case, reload with your carry ammo and try again. If that second run gives you another line of holes, you need to have your sights regulated (adjusted) to hit to point-of-aim. If the line is moving to the right of center, for instance, it means that your gun shoots to the right and needs to have the sights adjusted to bring the impact point to the left. Measuring the average distance between holes will give you a figure that will help you (or your gunsmith) move the sights an appropriate amount.

If the holes form a pattern other than a line, it's more than likely you're the cause. If the holes make a circular or spiral shape, it's likely that you're steering the gun in a certain direction — usually because your grasp is weak and allowing your trigger finger to move the gun as the trigger is compressed. If you're extremely consistent this can also result in a straight line pattern, but I've found that someone with this

issue is usually very inconsistent, hence the circular or irregular look to the pattern.

"Grabbing" the trigger, that is trying to get a shot off quickly as you try to hold the sights still, will usually result in alternating hits and misses to either the low-right or low-left; you'll have a couple of distinct groups of 2-3 shots each. Again, if you were extremely consistent it could look like a straight line, but what I said above still holds: if you have this problem you're probably not very consistent to begin with.

If the shots are just random, this is usually because you're not paying close attention to controlling sight movement on the target spot or your trigger control is inconsistent. Go back and reshoot the Moving Point Of Aim drill several times to hone your ability to let the gun move as much as it wants, as long as it's within the target area.

It's possible to have a combination of issues, and sometimes a random pattern can be caused by a combination of unadjusted sights and your own inconsistencies. I've had cases where I corrected a student's control issues, only to have a pattern of lines show up! The technique deficiencies were masking the gun problem.

## Special notes

You'll find this exceptionally difficult if your eyesight is at all diminished. I suggest reading the chapters on sight and sighting in either of my previous books, "Defensive Revolver Fundamentals" or "Defensive Pistol Fundamentals," for a full discussion of how to work around that limitation.

## NOTES

_____

_____

_____

_____

_____

_____

_____

_____

_____

## DRILL NAME:
## GOING THE DISTANCE

### Purpose

One of the pieces of data that comes out of the research of renowned defensive shooting instructor Tom Givens is the very occasional need for longer-range shooting skills in defensive encounters. (Some might argue that it in fact shows the relative *lack* of need for long distance shooting skills!) What Tom found is that shootings beyond about 10 yards are a very small percentage of total incidents, but they do happen and being able to hit at extended distances has proven valuable in some of the cases he studied.

How far is "long distance" in the scheme of things? Tom's work showed that 25 yards is getting to be on the edge of plausibility, and 50 yards is really the outer limit of long range for a handgun (beyond that point bullet drop starts to become a big issue in being able to place accurate rounds on target).

As it happens, problems shooting at these ranges are usually (barring an equipment issue, which the Chasing Precision drill will help you diagnose) psychological in nature. The increased distance is a powerful de-motivator, and the purpose of this drill is to show you that it's really no different than any other shooting challenge: it comes down to basic technique, nothing more!

It's important that you absorb the lessons of the Moving Point Of Aim drill before doing this drill.

### Rounds needed

Shooter's discretion; I've rarely had a student shoot more than 5 or 6 rounds at any given distance, but once you experience the feedback that comes from hitting a reactive target it can be a little hard to stop.

### Target

This is best done with some sort of reactive target that provides either audio or visual feedback (such as a steel plate or Pepper Popper). It can be done with a paper target, but the lack of feedback makes it impossible to use real-time technique correction to maximize the learning value. In classes, if we can't find a steel target we usually skip this drill because the instantaneous feedback is important to analyzing proper technique.

### Description

It's quite simple: set the target out at 25 yards to start. Extend on target, let your sights move within the

**This is really just a Press-Out drill at longer range, but it's a lot more fun!**

target outline just as you learned from the Moving Point Of Aim drill, and press the trigger for one shot. Evaluate whether you hit or missed. If you missed, immediately correct the problem by applying more of your skill. Concentrate on watching the sights move on the target and apply increasing pressure to the trigger without thinking about doing it. Bullet drop won't be an issue at this distance, so if you're missing it's your lack of application of skill.

Once you prove to yourself that you can hit the target a couple of consecutive times, try it from the holster: draw, extend out to target, take just enough time to let the sights "wobble" on the target, and press the trigger swiftly and smoothly. You'll notice this is really just a Press-Out drill at longer range, but it's a lot more fun!

When you can make consistent hits from the holster just as your gun reaches full extension (without any protracted settling time — what hunters used to call a "snap-shot") move the target back to 50 yards and repeat the entire drill from the beginning.

You can shoot beyond 50 yards, but you'll need to compensate for bullet drop. Every 5-yard increment past that point will, depending on the cartridge and bullet weight, make dramatic differences in impact point. The drill becomes less about application of physical skill and more about predicting the bullet's trajectory, and really has very little to offer to the defensive shooting student.

## Scoring/evaluation

A reactive target pretty much scores itself as hit or miss. If you're missing, you need to identify the cause; make sure that you're controlling the gun's "wobble" and always keeping the sights within the target area; make sure you have a solid grasp; make sure that you're concentrating on keeping the sights moving inside the target and not on pressing the trigger. If you find you have issues, go back and repeat the Moving Point Of Aim drill to remind yourself of the technique.

## Variations

If you have a range that will allow it, you can take a full six-pack of pop cans, shake them, line them up on a sawhorse and use them as your targets. There is something motivating and fun about exploding a pop can with a bullet, and the value of positive reinforcement on the learning process is undeniable, but be responsible and clean up after yourself! (Wasteful? I don't think so — sugary soft drinks aren't really good for you anyhow.)

**NOTES**

## DRILL NAME: STRONG-ARMS TACTICS

### Purpose

The reality of defensive shooting is that you won't always be able to get two hands on the gun. It's best, of course, if you can get two hands on the gun, but that's not always possible. You might be holding your child; you might be sweeping your spouse to cover behind you; you might be on the phone with 9-1-1; you might be holding a flashlight; you might be opening a door; or your other hand or arm might be injured. There are a lot of reasons that your other hand might be busy doing something relevant to the situation, enough so that you need to shoot your handgun with one hand.

Most of the drills for shooting with one hand are stylized affairs designed to develop the ability to shoot in situationally unrealistic scenarios. What I mean by that are the contrived stances and hand positions to maximize physical control, positions that take both time and require that the other hand have nothing else it needs to do, to make them possible. See the problem? If your other hand was available you'd get that onto the gun instead! Remember that the reason you're shooting with one hand is because the other hand is already busy doing something else, which means that its position (and your stance) are determined not by what is mechanically ideal but by what the environment dictates. A realistic one-hand shooting drill looks very unlike what you see in competition.

The goal of this drill is to give you practice in responses that are applicable to the plausible situations in which you might find yourself. I don't practice cradling a child, for instance, because I don't have children; I don't practice getting my spouse behind me, because she's armed whenever I am and will likely be an active participant in our defense. I do practice things like holding a flashlight or simulating a wounded arm, because those are the plausible situations I face (among others).

Before you do this drill, you need to identify what kinds of situations you could face which would cause you to need to shoot with only one hand. Think about them and acquire whatever props you need (flashlight, phone, etc.).

When you're doing these drills make sure that you don't adopt a one-hand-only-specific stance. Use the stance you're accustomed to and simply drop the support hand. Extend the shooting hand out as far as you physically can, rotate your shoulder forward to get more weight behind the gun, lock the elbow and wrist, and tighten all of the muscles in your arm. This will give you the maximum recoil control over the gun and still be consistent with all of the other practice you've been doing.

This drill can be done from the ready position (simulating a home defense response) or from the holster. I recommend that you practice both ways.

### Rounds needed

I recommend that you allot a certain percentage of your overall practice ammunition in any given session to this drill. How much a percentage? It depends on you and your environment; if you have small children or a spouse who doesn't carry, you'll probably want to spend more time with this drill than someone who's single and without kids. For most people, I'd say around 15-20% of your practice time and ammunition is reasonable; for those with kids or unarmed spouses, perhaps 25-30%.

### Target

I prefer the LE Targets #CFS-BSP for this drill. I find the small circles on this target to be quite useful for honing technique.

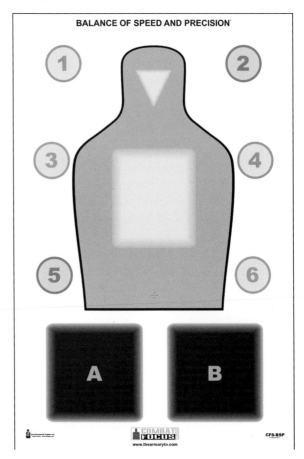

**LE Targets #CFS-BSP**

## Special equipment

Props as needed/applicable; a 10-lb sack of flour or sugar makes a dandy substitute for a small child; a 20- or 25-lb sack of livestock or pet feed works well to simulate larger kids.

## Description

This drill uses many of the elements of the Press-Out drill. You'll need to focus on physical control of the gun: full extension of the shooting arm; locking the shoulder, elbow and wrist as rigidly as possible; tightening muscles in the forearm; and especially your optimum grasp pressure (this is why I suggested that you do the Squeeze Me drill one-handed). Pay particular attention to your trigger press so that it doesn't affect the alignment of the gun on target.

Shoot at a realistic distance; for concealed carry that's typically around 3-5 yards, but for home defense it might be the length of your safe room.

**Stage 1:** For this first Stage, you're going to simulate an injury that forces you to shoot one-handed. Let your support arm simply hang, to your side or to the front, without muscle tension. Fire one round at the chest-sized area of the target, bring back to the ready position, and extend again for the next round. Watch the recoil pattern of the gun, particularly on your first rounds, and notice how tensing the muscles in your arm greatly reduces the muzzle flip. Repeat perhaps 5-6 times, enough to allow you to sort out what you need to do to make those hits.

**Stage 2:** Repeat, but this time fire multiple (3-5) rounds at that upper chest area of the target. You'll notice that your balance of speed & precision is very different than when you're using two hands. To be able to shoot rapidly and still get hits, you'll find that you need to exert far more muscular control over the gun than you might normally; you'll find that you'll need constant muscle tension in the shooting arm and hand to make every shot an accurate hit. Even so, you'll still be slower than you would using two hands — which illustrates why it's better to shoot two-handed if the circumstances allow it. Come back to the ready position between strings of fire and allow yourself to rest there for a few seconds before resum-

**Holding a flashlight is a realistic scenario for one-handed shooting.**

**If you have children, shooting while holding a simulated child is likely to be an important skill to practice.**

ing. Repeat several times.

**Stage 3:** Do the same thing, except this time integrate those props that you're likely to encounter in your environment: the child substitute, flashlight, cell phone, etc. Hold the prop in a realistic way (phone to the head, child held in your weak-side arm against your chest, flashlight to one side of the head and pointing at target, etc.). Do this several times with each prop.

**Stage 4:** Go back to the procedure in Stage 1, but this time use one of the small circles on the CFS-BSP target. One shot per extension, focusing on getting the hit inside the circle. Repeat 6-8 times, or until you can get consistent hits inside the circle.

**Stage 5:** The same procedure as Stage 3, but this time re-holster after every string of fire. Draw one-handed and fire multiple rounds into the chest area of the target. Reholster and repeat. (If your holster doesn't allow you to insert the gun using one hand, you need a safer holster. In a defensive shooting you may be required to reholster with only one hand, and a holster that collapses won't allow that. A holster that requires the use of two hands is also dangerous because it's almost impossible to get the gun in with-

out pointing it at yourself.) Repeat 4 to 6 times.

## Scoring/evaluation

100% hits. Just as when shooting with one hand, if the hits are clustered close together it shows that you can shoot faster than you've been doing. If you have misses, it indicates a lack of control; pay closer attention to muscle tension and grasp pressure.

A very common issue when shooting one-handed is to find shots landing high left or high right (depending on whether you're shooting with your right or left hand; the shots move away from the hand you're using). That's because the gun actually starts recoiling while the bullet is still in the barrel; if the muscles on the back side of your arm aren't tensioned properly, it will let the gun recoil excessively to one side and throw those shots wide. You'll probably see a small change in windage when shooting one-handed, but if it's extreme your muscle control is lacking. Try again, this time paying attention to tensioning those muscles for recoil control.

## Special notes

You can also do this drill weak hand only, but the only acceptable reason to shoot weak handed is because your strong hand has been injured. Do not draw from the holster; start with the gun in the weak hand and simulate the strong hand being injured. Fire single shots until you're comfortable with your control, then proceed to multiple shot strings. Weak hand shooting is so uncommon as to be rare, and I suggest no more than 5% of your time be spent on weak hand drills — and that's being generous, I think.

## NOTES

_____

_____

_____

_____

_____

_____

_____

# CHAPTER TWELVE

# DRILLS WITH A PARTNER

**DRILL NAME:**
**BALANCE OF SPEED & PRECISION**

## Designer

Rob Pincus/I.C.E. Training

## Purpose

One of the basic concepts in shooting is that of the balance of speed & precision. It's not a new concept, but it's one that hasn't really been talked about much in the world of defensive shooting until just a few years ago: the faster you shoot, the less precision you'll be able to achieve; to shoot to a greater level of precision requires that you apply more skill and control, which takes more time. This is something most shooters know intuitively, even if they're not aware they know it, because they'll slow down when they need to make a difficult shot and speed up when the shot isn't so difficult.

Knowing what your balance is in any given situation allows you to deliver the right amount of preci-

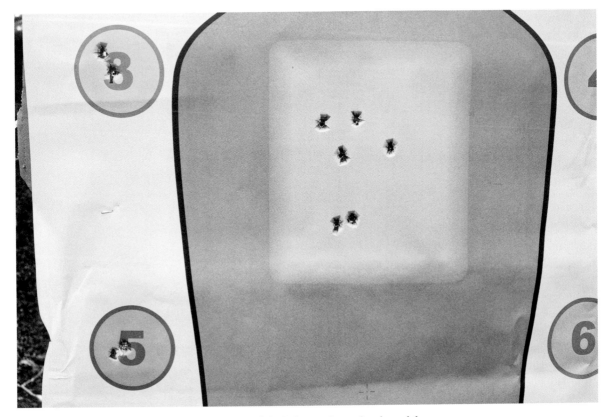

This shooter has a very good grasp of the concept of the balance of speed and precision.

sion, at the right amount of speed, and be able to hit the target (make accurate shots). Shooting to a greater level of precision than needed may take time that you don't have, but not shooting to the precision that the target requires might mean that your shots don't land in an area likely to cause incapacitation — and the fight isn't ended as soon as it could be. Understanding what that balance is under a variety of circumstances is crucial to mounting an efficient and effective defense. (For a more thorough discussion of this topic, please check out either of my previous books: "Defensive Revolver Fundamentals" or "Defensive Pistol Fundamentals.")

The Balance of Speed & Precision (BoSP) is the basic drill used by Rob Pincus in his Combat Focus Shooting program, and is designed to teach you what you need to do in varying circumstances to deliver accurate shots as fast as you can shoot. The only way to do this is to experience shooting under the widest range of circumstances possible, without being able to plan your strategy ahead of time. The goal is to be able to deliver the correct balance on demand, without foreknowledge of the circumstances under which you are going to shoot. This drill helps you to do that by making those circumstances as random as possible.

The idea is simple: targets of varying sizes (and later at varying distances), which your training partner calls at random, give you the opportunity to recognize the balance of speed & precision needed. This forces you to slow down when delivering shots that require greater precision, and allows you to shoot faster when the precision demands aren't as great.

This is also an extremely flexible drill with many possible variations. It is one of my favorites.

## Rounds needed

No fixed number; I recommend that you use at least 2-3 magazines per repetition to maximize the time spent on the drill. This is a drill that definitely benefits from uninterrupted activity.

## Target

The LE Targets #CFS-BSP was designed specifically for this drill, though you can also use the #SEB or the #KRT-1.

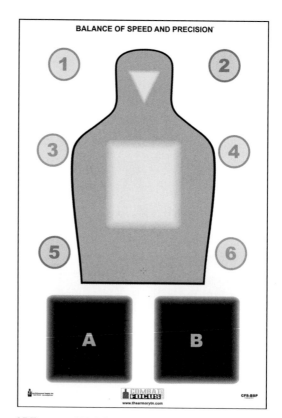

LE Targets #CFS-BSP

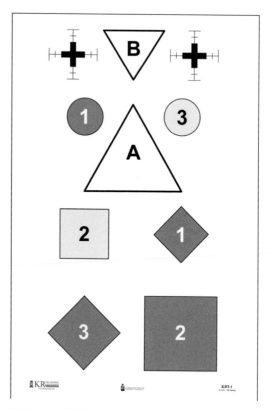

LE Targets #KRT-1

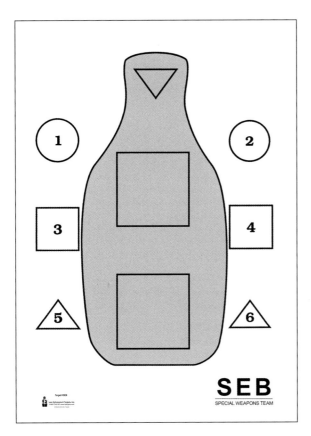

**LE Targets #SEB**

## Description

For your first experience with this drill you'll want to put the target at a realistic defensive shooting distance: around 3 yards to start. You'll be using two target zones on the CFS-BSP target: the center-chest rectangle and the small circles with numbers. As the chest rectangle gets shot up you can substitute one of the black boxes as the chest-sized area. You may shoot from the ready position or from the holster.

The drill is deceptively simple. There are two commands: the first signifies that you are to fire a random number of rounds — between, say, two and five — at that chest rectangle. I recommend you and your partner use the word "UP!", as it's unambiguous and easy to hear even with muffs on. The second command will be a number, which tells you to fire ONE round at the circle containing the number.

You need to always shoot as fast as you BELIEVE you can get the hits. This is important to the learning process because, as you learn just how fast you can get those hits, you adjust your expectations. This means that you learn what your own balance is on that target at that distance and internalize that knowledge.

Your training partner is to mix up, at random, which call he makes. In general, about 70% to 80% of the calls should be "Up!" with the remainder being one of the numbers. You must caution him not to make his calls in a pattern — that is, if you really want to learn what this drill is capable of teaching you!

Your balance of speed & precision changes with distance, so once you have a good grasp of what it takes to hit both the rectangle and the small circles step back a couple of yards and start again. Do this until you reach a distance of about 10-12 yards, which is getting to be the edge of the most common self-defense shooting distance. If you have a good grasp of your balance (and of the concept itself), you should find yourself slowing down a little each time the distance increases, but the accuracy of your shots should not change. The goal is always to make the hit inside of the target area.

## Scoring/Evaluation

Misses are common for most people at the start of the drill, but by the end you should be hitting every target 100% of the time without your shots being clustered.

In general, if you're missing it's likely a sign that you're shooting too quickly. There can be other causes, like an insufficient grasp or shooting while the arms are still extending, but a non-specific pattern of misses is a good sign you're simply shooting beyond your skill level at that target at that distance. Slow down.

If the shots on the chest rectangle are closely spaced, especially if they're in the center of the rectangle, then you're shooting more slowly than you need to be. I find that my students often do this because they try to use a classic sight picture on a large target at a short distance, where they really don't need to, or they're so used to the idea of smaller groups being "better" that they never try to shoot faster. If you understand your balance of speed & precision (for this target and distance) you should see an even distribution of shots within the target area.

The first few times you shoot this drill don't be surprised to see either lots of misses (shooting too fast) or really tight groups (shooting too slowly). As you get a grasp on the concept you should see that change to a good distribution of shots in the target but with no misses. That's the indication that you have reached your balance — for now!

## Variations

As mentioned, there are many variations and permutations possible. Here are a few I use:

1) Load your magazines between 40% and 60% of capacity. This forces reloads more often, giving you a chance to experience reloading under more realistic circumstances. Very often the shots immediately after the reload will be done much faster than the ones before and will very often miss the target entirely; you need to instruct your partner to watch for these and bring them to your attention, to remind you to think about your balance when you start shooting again.

2) Once you've experienced the drill at distances between 3 and 10 yards, instruct your training partner to mix up the range. Your partner could, for instance, have you shoot a few strings of fire at 3 yards, then have you back off to 7 and start the drill all over again. From there perhaps do some work at the 5-yard mark and then shoot some from 10 yards. The idea is to change the distance to give you experience at all ranges, which encourages the linkage between what you recognize (the distance and target size) and what it takes to hit that target (your application of skill and the resulting BoSP).

There is a more dynamic version of this variation later in the book, along with whole category of variations called "cognition drills."

## NOTES

_____

_____

_____

_____

_____

_____

_____

_____

_____

_____

_____

_____

# DRILL NAME: MOVING POINT OF AIM - PARTNER VERSION

## Designer

Unknown (though I learned it from an instructor named Georges Rahbani).

## Purpose

As I pointed out in the solo version of this drill, no one — not even Olympic shooters — holds a gun perfectly still. Your gun is always moving, and the difference between them and you is that their guns move less. The key to shooting smaller or more distant targets, or even precisely controlling hits when you're forced to shoot around innocents (which is often the case in home invasion scenarios) is understanding and learning to control that movement.

As I pointed out, most defensive shooting incidents don't require great precision shooting but there is a small (but definable) number that do. Being able to shoot to whatever level of precision you might plausibly need becomes a useful skill to develop. If I had to credit one drill that has given me that skill and the confidence that comes from knowing how to shoot to any level of precision, it would be this one.

This partner version of the drill helps your ability to deliver precision shots by allowing you to come to terms with the gun's movement, learn how to control it, and how to deliver precision shots even when you don't know exactly when you'll be asked to shoot.

This version's unpredictability forces you to concentrate on the gun, not the shooting. Having a surprise fire command helps you to place accurate shots when you're not expecting to need to shoot — which is very much like many defensive shooting incidents. It is important, however, that you have some experience with the solo version of this drill (detailed in the previous section).

## Rounds needed

The value of the drill diminishes with fatigue, and don't let the simplicity of the drill fool you — it can be very fatiguing. I would suggest no more than 30 rounds total, 6 on each target. If you're new to the drill (or to shooting in general), you might want to cut each repetition into two strings of 3 rounds each.

## Target

I like to use the LE Targets #VB-52 for this drill. Start

at the largest circle, and with each repetition move to the next smaller circle.

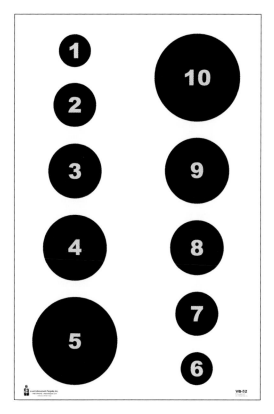

**LE Targets #VB-52**

## Special equipment

None.

## Description

Set the target at 3 yards. Stand with your gun loaded, at extension (in your preferred firing stance) and aimed at the center of the largest circle with your finger on the trigger. Your partner will say "Move," which is the command for you to consciously move the gun all over the inside of that circle. Concentrate on keeping the gun within the circle, never letting yourself drift outside of its boundaries. At some random point your partner is to use the "UP!" command, at which you immediately and without stopping the gun press the trigger swiftly back and fire one shot. Continue moving and wait for the next fire command. When you get tired, come back to the ready position and rest.

When you extend out for the next repetition, index on the next smaller circle; your partner then repeats the entire string of fire. Do this again on each of the remaining targets for a total of 60 rounds.

## Scoring/evaluation

Pass/fail; all shots must be hits inside the area of the target on which you're aiming. The great thing about

This drill is great for those with flinching issues. Having someone else focus on the timing of the shot, and leaving it as a surprise, forces you to really pay attention to something other than pulling the trigger.

this drill is that there are really only three possible reasons for a miss (assuming you understand what a sight picture looks like, of course). Either you deliberately (if unconsciously) stopped the gun to "grab" the shot; you didn't concentrate on keeping the gun aligned inside the target area at all times; or you didn't press the trigger smoothly. Fix whichever problem it is and try again.

## Variations

For shooters who find this a little too easy, back off to 7 yards. I submit that you won't find it so easy any longer.

## Special notes

While the solo version of this drill is helpful to shooters who have flinching issues, as it forces them to focus on something other than the gun going off, this partner version is even more so. Having someone else focus on the timing of the shot and leaving it as an open surprise forces you to really pay attention to something other than pulling the trigger. The sudden nature of the commands eliminates the tendency to take time to line everything up perfectly, and you'll probably find that going back and doing a Press-Out drill results in faster accurate shots on extension.

## NOTES

_____

_____

_____

_____

_____

_____

_____

_____

_____

_____

# DRILL NAME: COGNITION DRILLS

## Designer

Rob Pincus/I.C.E. Training

## Purpose

As I mentioned in the description of the Balance of Speed & Precision drill, there are many variations possible. One group of such variations on that drill are collectively referred to as Cognition Drills, and their purpose is to help you get used to the idea of thinking before and as you're shooting. This idea of "decisional shooting," as noted trainer Claude Werner calls it, is an integral part of defensive shooting.

The concept behind a cognition drill is to give your mind something to focus on, something to think about or figure out, immediately before the need to shoot. Part of it is being able to think about what you're doing — "do I really need to shoot?" — and the other part is to force a non-cognitive ("subconscious," most people would call it) recognition of all the stuff you normally think about in practice.

For instance, when we're practicing we're thinking about just how we're going to complete our draw stroke, how hard we're going to grasp the gun, how to keep the gun in alignment as we press the trigger, our sight picture (if we need it), and a myriad other little details. We do this just before we're given the command to shoot. The cognition drill short-circuits this just a little bit, and if your skills have not been mastered — practiced to the point that they can be activated without your direct thought — you'll see that deficiency in the results.

What I typically see in students is that they'll shoot a standard drill perfectly, but as soon as they're asked to think about something other than the execution of a skill their performance drops off noticeably. The more complex the drill becomes, the more they have to think about, and the worse their performance becomes.

On the other hand, those who have done enough training and practice to really ingrain those physical skills usually do quite well. They're now free to train the other stuff, the thinking stuff, that they need to do in any attack response.

The cognition drill is completely dependent on your training partner's ability to stay one step ahead of you, and his/her willingness to play with your mind and create commands that you might not expect. Your partner's job is to give you things to think about, puzzles to solve or decisions to make, and to do so in such a way that you can't predict what's going to happen.

Cognition drills are the most creative type of shooting drills. What can be done is limited only by the imagination (and mischievousness) of the training partner.

## Rounds needed

Like the Balance of Speed & Precision drill, this benefits from longer uninterrupted periods of activity. I suggest at least 3 magazines or speedloaders. Be aware that this drill can be very mentally taxing, so I recommend that you not get wild and load up a dozen magazines — give yourself a break to refill magazines/speedloaders.

## Target

Anything, really, but the more options on each target the easier it is for the training partner to come up with things for the shooter to think about. I find I use the LE Targets #CFS-BSP most often, simply because of the number of combinations and variations in the sizes and types of target areas that can be combined.

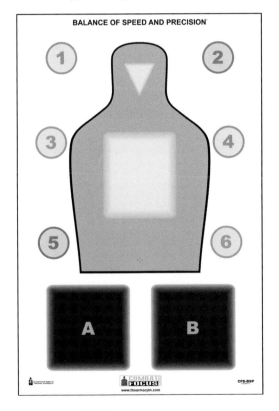

**LE Targets #CFS-BSP**

## Special equipment

None.

## Description

I recommend that you start at some plausible distance between roughly 3 and 7 yards; this isn't totally about marksmanship, it's about processing information prior to shooting and still being able to get the hits you need.

Establish with your training partner a standard shooting command, one that indicates you need to shoot multiple rounds to a chest-sized area on the target (I suggest using the command "UP!"). This is your baseline command, the one which should make up the majority of commands (70% or so) your shooting partner gives you.

The core reason for doing this drill is so that your partner is able to make up commands that indicate you should shoot something *other than* that chest-sized area. To do so, he may use commands containing numbers, letters, or math problems (i.e., the command "2 *plus* 2" means you shoot the target with the number 4 on it, while "2 *and* 3" means that you shoot the number 2 target AND the number 3 target). He may also use mnemonics (shoot the lettered target that matches the first letter in the word he calls); directionals (left, right, center, etc.); colors; shapes; or any combination of the above.

Truly creative training partners might say things like "how old is your second child" (shoot the target with the corresponding number); references to literature, music or movies; or anything else he can think of whose solution indicates what you should shoot. He should also occasionally drop in a problem whose solution matches nothing on the target, which is a good way to teach you not to shoot reflexively (and an important part of defensive training — not every problem is a shooting problem!).

Remember that the majority of calls should be the standard shooting command. This is to break up the expectation of shooting and make it harder to predict what's coming next, as well as getting you to switch immediately between reflexively shooting and needing to think whether you even should.

## Scoring/evaluation

Evaluation is much like the BoSP drill, but the goal is always 100% hits as fast as they can be had. You'll probably find that the first few times you run this drill you'll have more misses than you're accustomed to. This is because you're used to being able to think about *how* shoot rather than having to split your attention to thinking about *what* to shoot (or if you should shoot at all). If you have a great number of misses, or your shooting doesn't get better as you get used to processing information, it may be an indication that you need to go back to the earlier drills, particularly the Balance of Speed & Precision drill, and shoot them to help you learn to automate your physical responses. We want the application of your skills to be automated, but the decision to shoot (which is what cognition drills test) has to be made consciously!

## Variations

Virtually unlimited. You can add extra numbers or letters to the targets with a felt marker or spray paint; you can put up multiple targets and add directional commands to the others; if you and the shooter are programmers you can do all the numbers in octal; if you speak a foreign language you can make the decisional commands in a mixture of English and that language. Anything that causes the shooter to stop and think before drawing and shooting is fair game as long as it is safe.

## Special notes

For the training partner: Watch carefully for frustration in the shooter. Many times, particularly as the difficulty of the commands increases and the misses pile up, a shooter will become agitated and his gun-handling deteriorates — along with his hit percentages. This is particularly true with people who are highly trained but used to regimented and predictable drills, or with those who have a very sure opinion of their shooting ability. Such shooters may also have highly tuned firearms that malfunction at the worst time, which only adds to their growing irritation. If you see the shooter becoming frustrated, stop the drill and suggest a break. If you're a shooter yourself, you'll get your turn to experience those feelings when your roles are reversed!

## NOTES

_____

_____

_____

_____

_____

# DRILL NAME:
# SEARCH AND RESCUE

## Purpose

Assessment is a necessary component of self defense, and certainly of defensive shooting. In reality, you're always assessing your environment even if you're not aware of it; in the case of self defense, however, assessment is a more critical concept. "Situational awareness" is nothing more than conscious assessment: who's doing what, where they are, and so on. When a threat to your life presents itself, you continue to assess: do I need to shoot? Am I shooting in the right place? Do I need to shoot again? Do I need to stop shooting?

After you've been involved in a defensive shooting isn't the time to stop the assessment process! It may in fact be as important as the assessment you did before and during the incident. Is there another attacker threatening my life? Is there a police officer drawing his gun on me? Do I need to drop my gun? Is there anyone hurt? Do I need to move? All of these, and more, are possible and it's that continuation of the assessment process that needs to happen. It also needs to be practiced.

This part of the assessment process is really a search; you're searching your surroundings for things that are important relative to the incident. You're not searching for pop cans or shopping carts or water fountains, but rather for people and things that need your attention for some reason. It might be someone who is an additional threat, or it may be someone who needs your help. In some cases it might mean law enforcement who see someone with a gun (that would be you) and think you're the bad guy. In all of those cases you need to figure out your next move: shoot the threat, holster your gun and apply first aid, or drop your gun and put your hands over your head. You have to break your fixation on the task at hand (the person you just had to shoot) and look around, but look with a purpose.

When you finish a string of fire, whether in this drill or any other, before holstering you should include an area search: a continuance of the assessment process. Keep the gun in a ready position and turn your head; first to one side, as far around as you can, and then to the other side — again, as far around as you can. The goal is a 360-degree search, as the world exists all around you. Threats may come from behind (assuming you're not standing in front of a wall, of course) or from the side. Looking just ahead doesn't tell you, for instance, if the police are coming in response to a shots fired call. This is why a complete search is in a circle, with you in the center.

You may need to move your feet slightly to be able to manage a true 360-degree turn and still keep the gun pointed safely downrange.

You may need to move your feet slightly to be able to manage a true 360-degree turn and still keep the gun pointed safely downrange, and that's acceptable. (I'm right-handed, and find that I need to move my right foot back slightly to allow me to see to that side.) If you're supremely flexible you may not need to do that; so much the better! If you've been properly trained in depressed-muzzle ready position like Sul, you may be able to turn completely around safely.

This drill is designed to get you to think — to look around your environment and make decisions about the information you gather — when you've got a live gun in your hands. That's a critical defensive skill! It's also a necessary precursor to the Additional Threat Response drill.

## Rounds needed

This isn't a drill that you need to repeat; once you get the understanding and some practice in the search, you'll do it at the conclusion of any string of fire in most other drills. As such, a couple of magazines are sufficient then move on to a new drill.

## Target

Any, but the more complicated (the more options) the better. I like using the LE Targets CFS-BSP, or better yet the DT-2A, DT-2B, and DT-2C side-by-side to give lots of options.

## NOTES

_____

_____

_____

_____

_____

_____

_____

_____

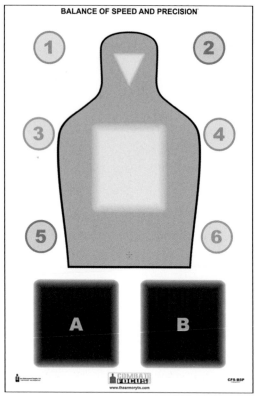

LE Targets #CFS-BSP

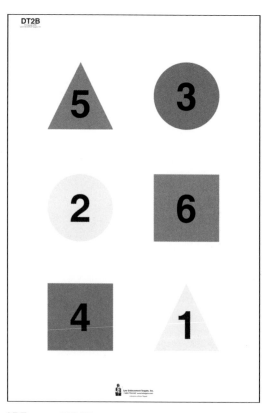

LE Targets #DT-2B

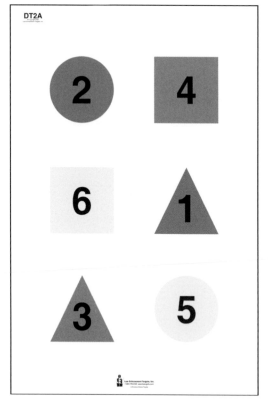

LE Targets #DT-2A

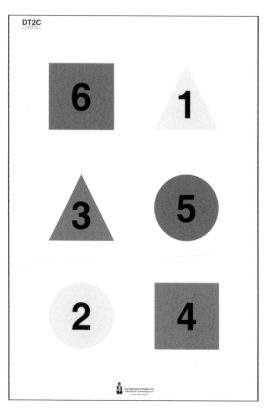

LE Targets #DT-2C

## Special equipment

None.

## Description

This drill should be shot at plausible distances, anywhere between 3-7 yards. Distance isn't important, but at the same time shouldn't be artificially long or short.

The training partner is to treat this drill like a Cognition Drill: make a large percentage of multiple-round, chest-area calls and an occasional call requiring the shooter to think a little more. After every string of fire the shooter needs to a 360-degree search of the area for some specific information.

It's during this search that the training partner is to do something that the shooter should be able to see if he/she is really looking. It might be something as subtle as having a hand in a pocket ("where was my left hand?") or the toes of one foot pointing in a certain direction. After the shooter finishes the search, the training partner asks whatever question is appropriate to determine if the shooter in fact really saw anything.

The training partner should move while the shooter is actually firing, so that the shooter doesn't get used to seeing him/her in the same place every time. It's even acceptable to do things like hide behind barricades, barrels or other cover, with just the tip of a shoe or part of a hand visible so that the shooter can find the partner if he's really looking and not just wagging his head.

This search test can (and should) be worked into every other partner drill in this book; the shooter, on the other hand, should be integrating a search after every string of fire, regardless of whether a partner is present.

## Scoring/evaluation

Just because this isn't a shooting drill per se doesn't relieve you of the need to make those hits! As in the other drills, if you're missing it's likely a sign that you're shooting too quickly and if your shots are clustered together you're probably taking more time than you really need to for that target. If you understand your balance of speed & precision (for this target and distance) you should see an even distribution of shots within the target area.

## Variations

Use a deck of cards or pre-made flash cards to simu-late that another "threat" has been found: the card should in some way tell the shooter which target is the additional threat, which he/she should shoot immediately. For instance, you can agree ahead of time that the card number indicates which numbered circle is the new "threat" to be shot. As the shooter starts searching, hold that card up (or put it in some conspicuous place for the shooter to "find").

You can also use other objects as target indicators, as long as you agree ahead of time what those indicators mean.

I particularly like using the combination of DT-2 targets to force the shooter to search each one to discover if there's another combination that matches what the training partner called — and thus needs to be shot as well.

## Special notes

For the training partner: You need to watch carefully that the muzzle stays pointed in a safe direction while the shooter is doing the search. On the range we need to observe safety procedures that might be different in the "real world," and the only generally safe direction in this environment is downrange. The shooter needs to keep the gun pointed downrange during this drill; if the muzzle drifts toward an unsafe condition, your should yell "STOP!," "MUZZLE!," or other pre-arranged command to indicate to the shooter that an unsafe condition exists.

## NOTES

_____

_____

_____

_____

_____

_____

_____

_____

_____

# DRILL NAME:
## ADDITIONAL THREAT RESPONSE

## Purpose

One of the big differences between the world of competition shooting and that of defensive shooting is how multiple threats are handled. In the competition context, the goal is to learn to move your eyes to the next target before swinging the gun to it; much time is spent practicing these transitions, to make them ever faster and gain an edge on the competition.

The problem with the "swinging transition" technique is that it only works when three conditions are met: first, that you know ahead of time what you need to shoot; second, that you know where the targets are; and, finally, that the targets don't move in relation to each other. If any of these is not met, the technique fails. As it happens, in the competition world all three are true, and in fact contests are often set up specifically to be sure all are true to give each competitor a "fair" chance.

Compare this to the world where you're in a convenience store and someone comes in to rob the place; whether you're a customer or behind the counter, you have a gun pointing a gun at you. While trying to figure out how you're going to deal with this immediate and dangerous threat you don't see the "shotgunner" who came in a little after the guy with the gun. You don't know ahead of time if there is an accomplice, or if there is which one of the other people in the store he might be (unless he too is pointing a gun at you the instant you recognize the primary threat). Since you don't know who he is, or even if he's there, you can't know where he is; and finally, once the first shot has been made everyone starts moving.

Even if you knew beforehand that he was there and where he was, while you're dealing with his buddy he's quite unlikely to simply stand there and wait for you to get to him. He's going to start moving too, and when you move your eyes to where he was to see where to swing your gun, he's likely no longer there. Now you need to look for him, and that's going to be difficult with your extended arms blocking half your view.

This (and more) is why the competition multiple target engagement looks nothing like the additional threat response of the defensive shooter.

How should you deal with additional threats in your immediate environment? First, you need to do something to break your fixation on your first target (threat) to allow yourself to be able to look around

'Swinging transition' technique is unrealistic given the way multiple assailant attacks actually happen.

and do a proper search for any additional threats you might face. You also need to clear your field of view so that you can see below your gun. (What if the accomplice ducked behind that short soft drink barrel display? You're not going to see him with your gun in front of your face or even lowered a little.)

The solution is to bring the gun into a ready position in front of your chest, at roughly the base of your sternum. This helps break your fixation and clears your field of view. As you bring the gun in toward your chest you can start looking — searching, really — for that additional threat (if there is one).

If you find another threat, someone who poses an articulable risk of death or grave bodily harm, you simply extend the gun back out to a shooting position. Now keep in mind that you may find that additional threat immediately, even before getting completely back into the ready position; in that case your extension may be very short and very fast. If you don't find that other threat until, say, you've searched to your side or back you'll have complete control of the gun and can then orient to that threat, extend, and shoot.

The key word to remember is "search." The additional threat response is, at its core, a search, and your gunhandling facilitates the search that you need to do.

The criticism of this method is that it's "slower" than the swinging transition technique. Yes, if the three conditions common to competition are met it's slower; the shooting contest world is different than the defensive shooting world. If they aren't met (and I hope I've established that it's a near-certainty they won't be in an actual encounter) it's going to be more efficient to do it this way.

This drill makes use of the visualization we talked about in a previous chapter. Out of context what you'll be doing seems pointless; it's only when you understand it in the context of its environment and conditions of use will it become clear why to do it this way. When any command is given, visualize the scene in as much detail as you can muster.

## Rounds needed

Depends on the training partner's calls, but generally figure on shooting a couple of magazines.

## Target

When teaching the basics of this drill I use the CFS-BSP target, utilizing the high-chest area and the two black squares below.

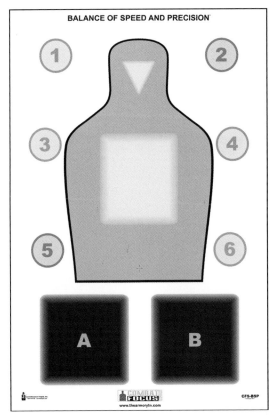

**LE Targets #CFS-BSP**

As you become familiar with the concepts you should switch to using the DT-2 series (preferably all three variants at once) to really mix up the potential for finding additional "threats."

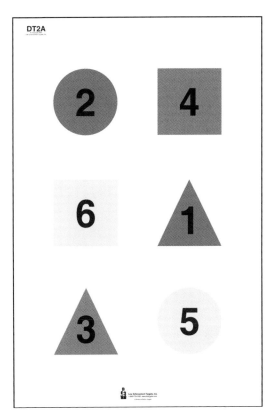

**LE Targets #DT-2A**

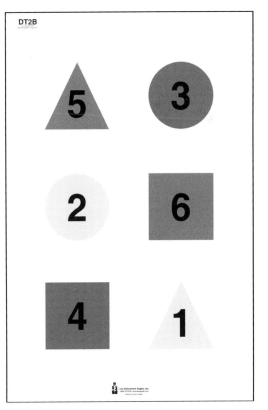

**LE Targets #DT-2B**

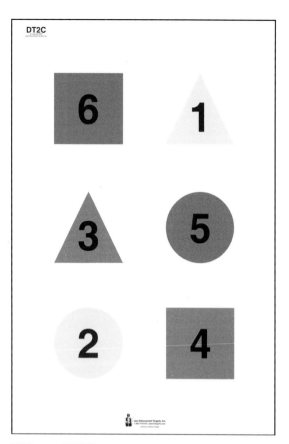

**LE Targets #DT-2C**

## Special equipment

None.

## Description

Start at a plausible defensive shooting distance; around 7 yards, maximum.

Your partner should start with some standard ("UP!") calls to shoot multiple rounds into the chest area, and at some point will call "Alpha" or "Bravo" — that's your signal that the threat is one of the large black squares. You'll shoot multiple rounds into those squares.

**Stage 1:** Visualize a large parking lot that you frequent; it could be your work, the grocery store you stop at several times a week, or maybe the parking lot at the movie theater you patronize every Friday night. See the lot, the cars around you, the buildings, and whether you're going in or coming out to your car. When any command is given visualize your attacker coming out from between the parked cars, weapon in hand. When you've identified the threat, shoot to deliver your rounds into the target area. When the call indicating multiple threats is given visualize your attacker and his incapacitation after you've fired your shots. As soon as your

Is there another target besides the #2 in the center? This variation really tests your ability to find and discern whether there are any other threats in your environment.

attacker is down in your mind's eye, bring the gun back into a ready position and start searching that parking lot for any possible threats; first to one side, then the other. Make sure to look completely around you, even in back (while keeping the muzzle pointed in a safe direction, of course!). As you come back around to the target from your search visualize the other black square as the second attacker, coming out from between some cars behind you; extend the gun out to a shooting position and neutralize that threat. This repetition helps show what happens when the second attacker has flanked you and come out of your blind spot; this kind of attack requires a search of greater angular displacement.

**Stage 2:** This time visualize being inside of a building with which you're familiar. It could be your office; the convenience store where you buy your coffee; the bank where you deposit your weekly paycheck; and so on. Visualize an attacker inside this building and use the same procedures you did in the first repetition. This time, rather than the second attacker having flanked you, visualize that he is in close proximity to the first attacker (say, behind a desk or a snack food display) and has engaged you to protect his buddy. After the first attacker has collapsed in your imagination and you simultaneously start your search as you bring the gun back to a ready position, you find him very quickly (because he isn't that far, in angular measurement, from the first threat). Immediately re-extend and fire multiple shots until he, too, collapses. This repetition happens much more quickly than the first, because your search has ended even before you got the gun back into the ready position.

This should clarify why the "swinging transition" technique so popular in the shooting games really doesn't bear any resemblance to the way criminals really behave, and why your technique for dealing with them needs to be different than the technique you use to shoot multiple, identical cardboard targets.

## Scoring/evaluation

Marksmanship really isn't the point of this drill, but at the same time you should be paying attention to your balance of speed & precision. It's not unusual to see misses, especially on the additional threats, usually indicating that the shots were made before the gun was fully extended in a shooting position.

## Variations

If your range allows it, use two targets and place them 8 to 12 feet apart. If you are at a range that allows shooting in a 270-degree arc, placing one in front of you and one on a side berm is helpful to better visualize angular displacement.

Use the DT-2 series and have your partner use target calls like those in the Rotation Drill. The idea is to mix them up; sometimes the command will be for a target area that only exists on one target, but sometimes it could exist on all three. Once you find the first threat, you'll need to search all of the targets to make sure that there are no others. This variation really drives home the need to make a search of your environment.

## Special notes

Training partner: Watch the muzzle carefully as the shooter does his search; very often it will wander and point at things it should not. If that starts to happen, yell "MUZZLE!" to indicate to the shooter that he's drifting. Also make sure that the shooter isn't just "wagging" his head very quickly; you want to see him/her really looking, really searching, for that other threat.

## NOTES

_____

_____

_____

_____

_____

_____

_____

_____

_____

_____

## Designer

Paul Carlson at Safety Solutions Academy (inspired by a drill from I.C.E. Training)

## Purpose

The limitation of most defensive shooting drills is that they don't change very much. By that, I mean that they don't have varying conditions as part of their structure. In fact, most drills are designed to be done in exactly the same way, every time, so that the shooter can compare results from past practice. This is the shooting-as-an-athletic-endeavor approach: we want to compete with ourselves or others, so we make the drills consistent and "fair."

The problem with applying this idea to the defensive shooting world is that lethal attacks are neither consistent nor fair. If you're attacked tomorrow, for instance, it's quite unlikely that you know ahead of time how far away your attacker will be. You'll need to make an immediate decision, based on your past training and experience, to what level of precision you need to shoot and how fast you'll be able to achieve the necessary accuracy.

There's a problem, however. If all you've ever done is shoot the same drills at the same old distances, never having given yourself the opportunity (or the need) to make those important decisions based on what you observe, where is that mental database you need to apply your skills to this attack? In order to build that database you need to practice under constantly changing conditions, and the only way to do that is to vary conditions (like, in this case, the distance to the target) on a dynamic basis — that is, changing in a rapid and random manner as you're practicing.

This concept of constantly practicing something slightly different is called interwoven education, and it has a solid neurological framework: people do, in fact, learn faster if their learning stimuli are varied or interwoven. That's what this drill does. It efficiently exposes you to a random set of shooting challenges which forces you to assess information, make decisions, and apply the appropriate skills to deliver accurate hits to the target. It's best used as a tool to bring your skills together, and can be used to integrate new skills you've learned with those that you already know

in a more realistic, 360-degree environment.

## Rounds needed

It's a good idea to have at least 3 magazines or speedloaders per run of the drill to minimize downtime. More are better; the benefit of the drill is greatly increased by being able to experience many different distances in as short a time period as possible, and having more ammunition allows you to do that without pausing to refill everything.

## Target

The LE Targets #CFS-BSP is ideal for this drill; use the center-chest area to start, and as that gets shot up you can use the "A" and "B" boxes as a substitute.

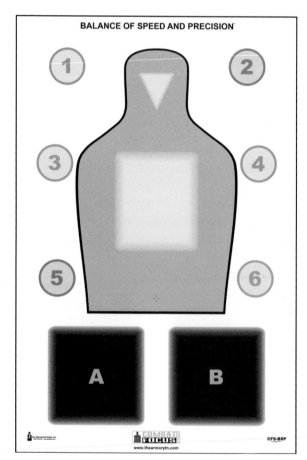

LE Targets #CFS-BSP

## Special equipment

None, though this drill does require a range that allows you to move back and forth relative to a fixed target and to draw from a holster (all shooting is done after a draw).

## Description

Start by marking minimum and maximum plausible defensive shooting distances from the target. I suggest no closer than 2 yards and no more than about 7 yards. You can use anything to mark those distances: a piece of masking tape on the floor, a soft drink can, or even just a piece of wadded-up paper.

Your training partner will walk the drill alongside you, and as you walk he's to carry on a non-related conversation (about the weather, your jobs, who's going to win the Super Bowl, or anything else that will help to distract you and make the shooting command less expected). He'll use these commands to indicate what he wants you to do:

- FORWARD: Walk casually toward the target (your partner needs to make sure that he doesn't allow you to walk past the close distance marker).

- BACK: Walk (facing up range*) toward the maximum distance marker (again, your partner needs to watch that you don't go past the marker).

- STOP: You are to freeze in place; do not complete any actions, such as reloading (this is a safety valve should you do something unsafe).

- UP!: The command to shoot a multiple but random number of shots into the center-chest area of the target.

*When a directional command is given, if it results in a 180-degree change of direction you're both to turn so that you face in the direction you're traveling. This is not a drill where you walk backwards!

The partner should give several movement commands for each shooting call; while you're moving, avoid looking at the targets — the idea is to force you to judge your distance to the target at the instant the shooting call is made.

Once you've completed the shooting command, re-holster and wait for your training partner's next movement command.

Your partner needs to consciously vary (randomize) the movement commands and the distance at which the shooting commands are given. The goal, remember, is to get you to recognize the distance at

The training partner needs to watch for this 'gaming' move; it's not a realistic response to an unknown stimulus and it's not safe.

which you need to shoot and recall the skills to shoot as fast as you can (and still make accurate hits) at that distance. Always stopping at one specific distance dilutes the value of the drill.

You and your training partner should do a "dry run" before loading up, to get each of you used to the commands. Once you're comfortable, load and have your partner start the drill.

## Scoring/evaluation

Ultimately, the goal is 100% accurate hits on all target calls. You may find that there are certain distances or combinations of calls that cause you to miss the target area; for instance, if your shots are accurate at the closer distances but you have missed shots at the longer distances, it's a good indication that you're either shooting too quickly or not applying enough physical control over the gun. If your shots at the close targets are clustered tightly together, it shows that you're shooting too slowly on those calls.

It's easy to allow yourself to shoot at one rate (one balance of speed & precision) at all the distances. It takes work to figure out what your balance is at any distance so that your shots are always "just right." That's what this drill is designed to do: to give you that constantly changing opportunity to shoot at your optimum balance of speed & precision.

## Special notes

If the training partner gives a shoot command while the shooter is facing away from the target, the shooter needs to fully turn to face the target before the draw is initiated. This is important: the shooter cannot start drawing the gun until squarely facing the target; if that happens, it's the training partner's job to give the STOP command and correct the shooter's mistake!

## NOTES

_____

_____

_____

_____

_____

_____

## DRILL NAME:
## THE DOUBLE BTR

### Designer

Paul Carlson (Safety Solutions Academy) & The Author

### Purpose

(This is an expanded variant of Carlson's BTR drill, and is presented here separately because there are significant changes in what the drill accomplishes and how the results are interpreted.)

As mentioned in the BTR Drill entry, a big limitation of most defensive shooting drills is that they don't change very much. By that, I mean that they don't have varying conditions as part of their structure. In fact, most drills are designed to be done in exactly the same way, every time, so that the shooter can compare results from past practice. This is the shooting-as-an-athletic-endeavor approach: we want to compete with ourselves or others, so we make the drills consistent and "fair."

The problem with applying this idea to the defensive shooting world is that lethal attacks are neither consistent nor fair. If you're attacked tomorrow, for instance, it's quite unlikely that you know ahead of time how far away your attacker will be or the size of the target area he presents to you. You'll need to make an immediate decision, based on your past training and experience, to what level of precision you need to shoot and how fast you'll be able to achieve the necessary accuracy.

There's a problem, however. If all you've ever done is shoot the same drills, with the same targets, at the same unvarying distances, you've never given yourself the opportunity (or the need) to make those important decisions based on what you observe. This makes it difficult to have that mental database you need to apply your skills to an attack. In order to build that database you need to practice under constantly changing conditions, and the only way to do that is to vary conditions (like target size and the distance to the target) on a dynamic basis — that is, changing in a rapid and random manner as you're practicing.

This concept of constantly practicing something slightly different is called interwoven education, and it has a solid neurological framework: people do, in fact, learn faster if their learning stimuli are varied or interwoven. That's what this drill does: it efficiently exposes you to a random and complex set of shooting challenges, which force you to assess information, make decisions, and apply the appro-

This drill benefits from a range that allows you to move back and forth relative to a fixed target and to draw from a holster (all shooting is done after a draw).

priate skills to deliver accurate hits to the target. It's best used as a tool to bring your skills together, and can be used to integrate new skills you've learned with those that you already know in a more realistic, 360-degree environment.

This drill allows the training partner, who is in control of the training experience, to vary both the size of the target and the distance at which you need to shoot in a constantly varying and (we hope!) unpredictable manner. It is best thought of as an advanced drill for those who have a good working understanding of the balance of speed & precision and have had some experience testing that understanding in some of the other drills.

## Rounds needed

It's a good idea to have at least 3 magazines or speed-loaders per run of the drill to minimize downtime. More are better; the benefit of the drill is greatly increased by being able to experience many different distances in as short a time period as possible, and having more ammunition allows you to do that without pausing to refill everything.

## Target

This drill requires the LE Targets #VB-52 (or a home-brewed equivalent).

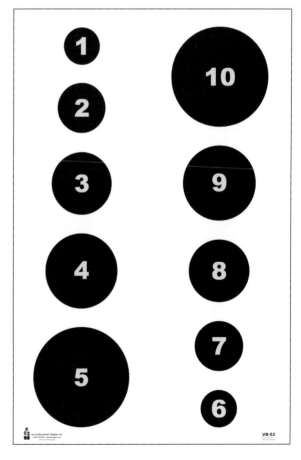

LE Targets #VB-52

## Special equipment

None, though this drill does benefit from a range that allows you to move back and forth relative to a fixed target and to draw from a holster (all shooting is done after a draw). If you are on an indoor range with retractible targets, your partner can simply run the target back and forth, stopping at appropriate distances.

## Description

Start by marking minimum and maximum plausible defensive shooting distances from the target. I suggest no closer than 2 yards and no more than about 7 yards. You can use anything to mark those distances: a piece of masking tape on the floor, a soft drink can, or even just a piece of wadded-up paper.

Your training partner will walk the drill alongside you, and as you walk he's to carry on a non-related conversation (about the weather, your jobs, who's going to win the Super Bowl, or anything else that will help to distract you and make the shooting command less expected). He'll use these commands to indicate what he wants you to do:

- FORWARD: Walk casually toward the target (your partner needs to make sure that he doesn't allow you to walk past the close distance marker).

- BACK: Walk (facing up range*) toward the maximum distance marker (again, your partner needs to watch that you don't go past the marker).

- STOP: You are to freeze in place; do not complete any actions, such as reloading (this is a safety valve should you do something unsafe).

For this drill, the shooting command will be a number corresponding to one of the target circles on the VB—52 target. If your partner calls "THREE!" for instance, you're to shoot a random number of rounds (say, between 2 and 4 rounds) into the #3 target circle.

*When a directional command is given, if it results in a 180-degree change of direction you're both to turn so that you face in the direction you're traveling. This is not a drill where you walk backwards!

The partner should give several movement commands for each shooting call. While you're moving, avoid looking at the targets — the idea is to force you to judge your distance to the target at the instant the shooting call is made.

Once you've completed the shooting command,

assess (do a 360-degree search), re-holster and wait for your training partner's next movement command.

Your partner needs to consciously vary (randomize) the movement commands and the distance at which the shooting commands are given, as well as the target sizes. The goal, remember, is to get you to recognize the distance at which you need to shoot, the level of precision which the target is demanding, and recall the skills to shoot as fast as you can and still make accurate hits on that target at that distance. Always stopping at one specific distance, or always using similar-sized targets, dilutes the value of the drill.

You and your training partner should do a "dry run" before loading up to get each of you used to the commands. Once you're comfortable, load and have your partner start the drill.

## Scoring/evaluation

This drill requires you to pay more attention to your shooting, and particularly to assessing as you shoot. Most of your evaluation needs to come from what you observe as you shoot, as it can be difficult to distinguish which factor made you miss which target after the fact. This is, in fact, as much a drill about assessment as it is shooting.

As in any drill, the goal is 100% accurate hits on all target calls with an acceptable balance of speed & precision (i.e., no misses but no tightly clustered shots, either). You'll know when you've achieved a balance when your shots all land within each target area, but don't present any obvious grouping.

You may find that there are certain distances or combinations of distance and target size that cause you to miss more often; for instance, if your shots are accurate at the closer distances (and/or larger targets) but you have missed shots at the longer distances or at the smaller targets, it's a good indication that you're either shooting too quickly or not applying enough physical control over the gun. If your shots at the closer or larger targets are clustered tightly together, it shows that you're shooting too slowly on those calls.

Occasionally I'll have a student who seemingly inexplicably hits smaller targets at the longer distances, but misses the larger targets up close. That's usually because they've decided that the larger, closer targets are "easy" and allow themselves to get lazy in terms of things like trigger control and proper grasp on the gun. At the longer distances and smaller targets, they know they're hard and really apply themselves. You need to pay attention to those fundamentals all the time, not just when you think you need to!

Two different runs of the drill - targets on left show shooter hasn't quite grasped the concept of the balance of speed and precision, while second run on right shows the lesson has been learned.

## Purpose

The reality of self defense is that sometimes you don't need to shoot. In fact, many times you probably shouldn't even have your hand on your gun until you've determined that you really need to! If you take a defensive shooting class, however, the drills are all designed to develop your ability to shoot rather than your ability to decide if you *need* to shoot.

The best way to develop that decision-making skill is to participate in scenario-based force-on-force ("FOF") training with role players and special training ammunition fired from special guns. The problem is that this kind of training is expensive, hard to find, and often too poorly run to gain any real benefit. For an entire class it's also time consuming and difficult to implement. The result is that the majority of the defensive shooting world sort of ignores this vital aspect of training.

This drill is an attempt to bring some of that decision-making into a standard range exercise. The idea is to keep you guessing as to what the next target will be, or if there even is a target. This is done by using three targets that are, at quick glance, very similar but different in detail, and moving you between them constantly. This, combined with some subtle manipulation by your training partner, randomizes the shooting challenge enough to force you to actually think and continually assess every time, rather than just reflexively drawing the gun and blazing away.

## Rounds needed

You'll need at least 3 full magazines or speedloaders; the more the better, as it allows you to keep moving and experiencing the decision-making aspects of the drill.

## Target

LE Targets DT-2A, DT-2B, and DT-2C (you'll need all of these).

## NOTES

_____

_____

_____

_____

Because the area of target precision is changing along with the distance, you should experience significant changes in your balance of speed & precision as you run through the drill. It's easy to allow yourself to shoot at one rate (one balance of speed & precision) at all the distances, sometimes without regard to the target size. If you notice yourself doing this, stop and regroup. Think about what you're doing, what you need to do to place shots inside the target area, and pay closer attention to analyzing your response for any given combination.

For most people, this turns out to be a very challenging drill, especially if the training partner is paying close attention to what he's doing.

## Special notes

If the training partner gives a shoot command while the shooter is facing away from the target, the shooter needs to fully turn to face the target before the draw is initiated. This is important: the shooter cannot start drawing the gun until squarely facing the target; if that happens, it's the training partner's job to give the "STOP!" command and correct the shooter's mistake!

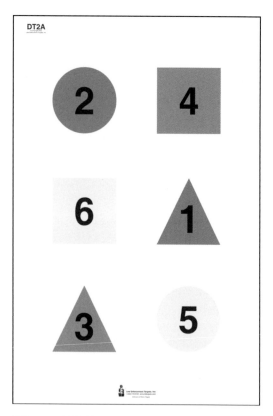

**LE Targets #DT-2A**

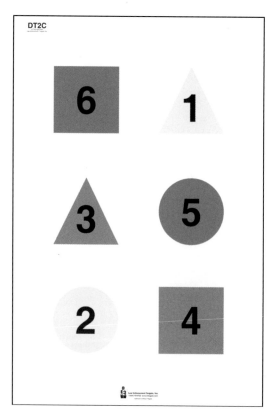

**LE Targets #DT-2C**

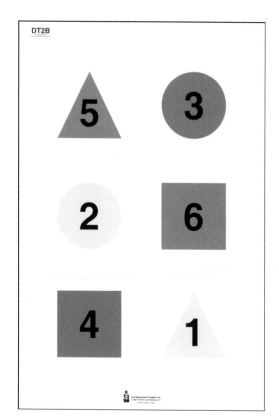

**LE Targets #DT-2B**

## Description

The targets are set up side by side; if the range allows, they should be place 2-3 feet apart. Distance to the targets can be any plausible defensive shooting distance, though I find 5-7 yards works best given the size of the target areas.

There are several types of target indications on the DT-2 series. Targets can be called by number, shape, or color. They can also be called as combinations: "red 3" or "yellow triangle" or "square 2." There are, as you can see, quite a few possibilities but there's a catch: not all combinations are on every target variant! Sometimes a combination will be on two of the variants, or sometimes they only occur on one variant. There are even a few combinations that occur on none of them.

Naturally, the normal Cognition Drill options of math problems, etc. are still open:

**Image 1: If and when you find a valid target, fire a random number (between 3-5) of rounds into that target.**

**Image 2: After your gun is holstered, turn and walk to the next target.**

Image 3: When you're in front of the next target turn your back to it and repeat the drill.

Image 4: There's a catch: not all combinations are on every target variant. Make sure there is a legitimate target prior to drawing your gun!

You'll start with your back to the first target. When your training partner makes a target call you need to flinch like you've heard a loud noise: bring your hands up in a protective posture. Only then may you turn around and find the called target. This is a safety measure, to ensure that you aren't starting to draw the gun at the same time your turn is initiated. (In reality, drawing a gun may not even be a correct response because you don't really know if a combination is on the current target!) This drill isn't concerned with turning fast or drawing as early as possible; it's about assessing information, finding and identifying a threat. Don't try to rush the turn to get faster — it's just not necessary!

If and when you find a valid target, fire a random number (between 3-5) of rounds into that target, then do a solid 360-degree search (remember the Search and Rescue drill?) before reholstering. After your gun is holstered, turn and walk to the next target (this is why it's called "Rotation"). When you're in front of the next target turn your back to it and repeat the drill.

This is a very difficult drill to "game," because it's hard to memorize all of the combinations and on which target variant they occur. (I recommend folding the target stock number, which is on the top-left corner, under when the targets are mounted to their frames. This hides the variant label so that you shooter won't know which one is where. This makes it doubly difficult to memorize the target layout.)

## Scoring/evaluation

This can be a very disorienting drill, and it's easy to miss even these generously-sized targets at the recommended distance. Part of it is because you'll get caught up in the decision making process and forget all about your shooting fundamentals, but also because the target shapes disturb your analysis of what the proper balance of speed & precision is at the distance you're shooting. The anxiety of not knowing ahead of time what you're going to shoot (or even if there is a legitimate target) tends to take your focus away from your job of hitting the target. Still, your goal needs to 100% hits inside of each target area. You should be assessing as you shoot, and if you see a miss made you need to immediately follow that up with a solid hit. Even good shooters tend to get very sloppy when faced with this drill, so you're in good company — but don't let that be an excuse for missing.

## Special notes

Training partner: The combinations that occur on each target can be found in the Targets chapter toward the front of the book. Use those listed combinations to occasionally throw in a call that isn't on the current target. Do not let the shooter stare at the targets after shooting. Keep her moving so that she can't easily predict what's next!

## NOTES

_____

_____

_____

_____

_____

_____

_____

_____

_____

_____

_____

_____

_____

_____

_____

_____

_____

_____

_____

# DRILL NAME: NO-SPRINT (RESTRICTED RANGE DRILL)

## Purpose

I've mentioned several times that one of the best ways to learn the concept of the balance of speed & precision is to practice shooting at different-sized targets or at targets from varying distances. The Balance of Speed & Precision drill (and its variants) and the Cascade drill work with the former, while some of the drills in the Partner section address the latter.

It's that varying distance to the target which is a problem on a lot of restricted ranges, particularly indoor ranges, because they don't allow for the kinds of drills — like Carlson's BTR or Double BTR — that best test that particular skill. The value of those drills is in not knowing, at any point in time, at what distance you're going to be expected to shoot and is lost when you can't change that distance "on the fly."

On a restricted range you don't have the constantly variable distances, but you can randomize the distances a little bit by using a couple (or several, if the range allows it and space is available) of targets set adjacent to each other laterally, but at different distances from the firing line. The targets ("back", "front", "middle") can then be called randomly and you'll have to instantly figure out what the balance of speed & precision is for that target at that moment.

Those ranges that have retrievable target hangers and defined lanes will be even more difficult to work with, but it can be done if you're allowed to use more than one lane (assuming no one else wants to use those lanes, of course — be sure to ask permission first!). You'd walk back and forth from lane to lane and your partner would make calls at random. This variation actually works quite well, but you need to ensure that you're completely square to the target before you begin drawing your pistol!

If the range doesn't allow drawing from the holster and uses retractable target frames, your training partner can simply run the target back and forth, and whenever he gives the firing command you shoot the indicated target starting from the chest-ready position. (Again, be sure to ask permission of the range operator before you do this; some may not allow you to play with their mechanisms in that manner.)

## Rounds needed

Whichever way you run this drill, I'd suggest shooting at least two, preferably three, magazines or speedloaders in order to get in a large number of repetitions.

## Target

To recreate the Carlson BTR drill for a restricted range, use the LE Targets #CFS-BSP.

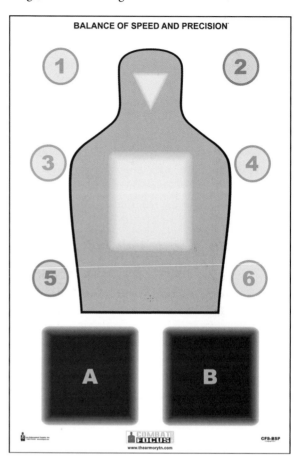

LE Targets #CFS-BSP

To recreate the Double BTR, use the #VB-52 target.

## NOTES

_____

_____

_____

_____

_____

_____

_____

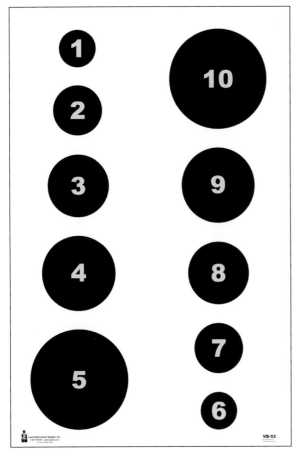

**LE Targets #VB-52**

## Description

First, go back and read the descriptions of the Carlson BTR Drill and the Double BTR Drill for important background and general procedures. You'll be adapting those concepts to a range where you can't move, so the targets need to.

If you're using fixed target stands or hangers, the targets should be arranged so that they're roughly double the distance from each other. The first target should be about 3 yards away; the second about 6; and the third around 12. These are not hard-and-fast distances, but simply a guideline.

If you're using fixed targets, when the command to fire is given move so that you're squarely in front of the indicated target and in line with it, then draw and shoot a random number of rounds (between 3 and 5) at the target. When you've re-holstered, take a quick look at the target before resuming the drill; check

where your shots landed. This is important feedback to establishing your balance at any given distance.

If you've elected to have your training partner run the target back-and-forth, establish minimum and maximum distances; I suggest 3 yards for the closest, and 12 yards for the farthest. Your partner should run the target back and forth at random, not always going to the minimum or maximum before reversing. When the target stops, your partner is to give the command to shoot.

## Scoring/evaluation

I'd encourage you to read the BTR drill descriptions for a more thorough discussion of target analysis, but as with most of the drills here you're looking for general patterns. If you find that at any given distance your shots are clustered close together, that's a sign you are shooting too slowly for that target size at that distance, and you should increase the pace of your shots. If you have misses, it's usually a sign that you need to apply more control over the gun — slow down just a bit.

Ideally, you should be shooting at a slightly different pace at each distance while still getting 100% hits that don't show signs of tight clustering. If you're shooting at the same speed all the time, it means you're shooting to quickly on some targets or too slowly on some. Look at the target carefully, and it will tell you which is the case.

## Variations

On extremely restricted ranges that don't allow drawing from the holster or rapid fire, use the small numbered circles on the CFS-BSP target, use distances between 3 yards and 7 yards, and fire one round per command from the ready position; if you miss, bring the gun back into the ready position, then extend out again and fire another shot.

## Special notes

If using fixed targets and moving between then, your training partner needs to make sure that you're not drawing the gun before being in front of and square with the target. Use a pre-arranged warning command ("muzzle!" works well) to indicate that you need to stop and correct yourself before continuing.

# CHAPTER THIRTEEN

# MAKING IT REAL: BASIC SCENARIO DRILLS

## DRILL NAME:
## HOME DEFENSE RETRIEVAL

### Purpose

In the training world we often say that there are only two safe places for your firearm: on your person or in a locked container. That is doubly true if you have children in your home; an unlocked, unattended gun is dangerous to curious children (even if your kids aren't curious, their friends are likely to be). The result of this realization is the common recommendation that you should always carry your gun at all times even when you're in your home. It's almost a point of

This drill is to give you practice getting to your safely stored home defense gun and readying it for action.

pride amongst the training cadre that they never take their guns off except to go to sleep.

The trouble with that line of thinking is that we don't always have our guns on us. If you're taking a shower, for instance, it's unlikely that you'll be wearing your gun. (Yes, I'm sure the super-ninjas out there have one within arm's reach at all times, but realistically it's out of your immediate control and should be secured in some manner.) It's possible that you could come out of that shower to the sound of breaking window glass, signaling an intruder.

You might also be one of those people who doesn't have a concealed carry license (in those jurisdictions where they're needed) or who works in a job where guns are forbidden. In either case, you're not likely to be packing when you come home after work and someone follows you into your house. It happens.

It shouldn't need to be said, but you're also not going to have your gun on when you're sleeping. (As I'm writing this, news of a self-inflicted gunshot is making the rounds; a fellow who slept with two guns *in his bed* rolled over one night and somehow managed to fire one of them, resulting in a wound to his pelvis! That's just one reason why you shouldn't have a gun with you when you go to sleep.)

In all of these cases your gun isn't in your immediate care and custody, and therefore should stored be in a secure, locked container, preferably one of the quick-access safes that are on the market. If something happens where you need that lethal force tool, you'll need to be able to retrieve it quickly and efficiently. Getting to the storage container and doing what's necessary to get into it and access the gun, under pressure, is a specific skill set that you really should train and rehearse before needing to do it for real.

Even if you don't have children and choose to stage guns in your home without the benefit of a locking container, you still need to practice getting to them, loading them, and getting into a solid shooting position/stance. Practicing that now would be a good idea, which is why this drill exists.

## Rounds needed

This isn't a drill where you shoot a lot of ammunition; this drill really is intended more to test your movement to and manipulation of your gun and/or its storage container. As a result, one full magazine per repetition will be more than sufficient, though I recommend having a second one stored with the gun to take with you in case you need to move away from the storage area.

I recommend that you run through this drill several times to embed the sequence of events firmly in your mind.

## Target

I suggest using the LE Targets #CFS-BSP, simply because of its general resemblance to the human silhouette. In reality you can use anything, including a paper plate. Again, this isn't as much about shooting as it is your physical access to the gun.

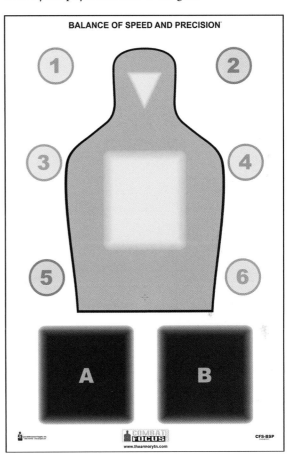

LE Targets #CFS-BSP

## Special equipment

A quick-access safe or a suitable substitute (a latching ammo can works well). You may also need masking tape or some sticks to set up a floor plan (cheap 1x2" lath works well). The range you use must allow you to move between some starting point and your gun, and it's best set up on a range where you can recreate your own floor plan on the ground or floor.

It doesn't take more than a few boards and some props to simulate the conditions under which you'll need to retrieve your defensive firearm.

While a training partner isn't absolutely necessary for this drill, having one to make your start signal random, unpredictable and somewhat realistic (like screaming, yelling, or perhaps even a board breaking to simulate a door being kicked in) is most helpful.

## Description

If the range allows it, use the masking tape or 1x1s to recreate the room in which you store your gun. Lay out the walls, the doorway, and perhaps any large furniture around which you need to navigate. Make them as true to scale as you can. (You can see where a large indoor range or outdoor shooting bay is best if you're trying to recreate a large bedroom.) Be sure to lay out any hallways down which you need to run to get to the "room."

Orient the "room" to the target so that you're in the same shooting position (relative to the rest of the room) from which you expect to mount your defense. If, for instance, your bedroom looks like this:

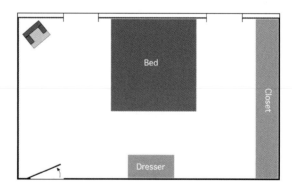

**If your bedroom looks like this...**

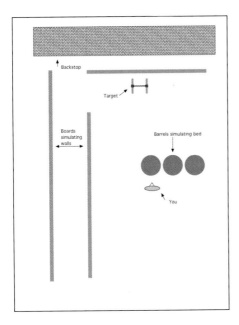

**...then your range layout would look like this (assuming you keep your safe under the bed).**

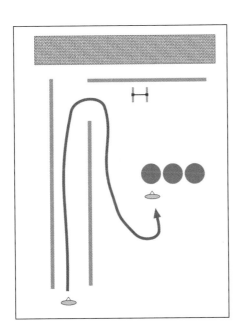

**Your movement through the completed "set" would look like this.**

On the command or the decision to start the drill, run into the room, retrieve your gun from the container, load it, and shoot the target multiple times in the center-chest area from a standing position. This is a drill to test your ability to efficiently retrieve your handgun from storage, nothing more.

## Scoring/evaluation

Even though this isn't really a drill about shooting, don't allow yourself to get complacent or sloppy with your shooting. You still need to hit the target with all rounds inside the target area. If you're not, that means you're either lazy or don't have a complete understanding of the fundamentals; if the latter is true, go back to the previous drills and practice some more.

## Special notes

You can use a variation of this even on restricted indoor ranges, with the range manager's approval, of course. Start outside the range room, with perhaps a display counter in the way, and on the command get around the obstacles, through the range door(s) and to your "safe" on the bench in your shooting lane. It won't be as realistic as recreating your own room, but it will give you some experience in getting to the gun even after getting around furniture and through doorways. In these cases it's best to leave a partner inside the range to watch your gun and prevent someone from walking off with it.

## NOTES

_____

_____

_____

_____

_____

_____

_____

_____

_____

_____

## DRILL NAME: SUDDEN RESPONSE

### Purpose

This drill addresses two separate and important concepts in defensive shooting.

First is the need to be able to think and function with a gun in your hand — to be prepared for action while at the same time being able to process the information that's flowing into your brain. It's one thing to stand in front of a target, draw on command and shoot; it's a different thing altogether to have that gun in hand, keep it pointed in an appropriate direction, and carry on a conversation with the 9-1-1 operator whom you've called to report that bad guy in your midst.

What happens if, while you're trying to tell the operator where you are and what's going on, the bad guy decides to run at you — or break in the door of your bedroom? Can you efficiently switch tasks from proactive (calling for help) to reactive (dealing with that immediate threat)?

In a complex situation like that it's easy — too easy — to get fixated on one thing: the gun, to the exclusion of the call for help; or the call for help, to the exclusion of keeping track of the threat. We don't often practice this "juggling" of duties, and that's a mistake. This is the kind of scenario where things can go very wrong: for the innocent who comes around the corner when you were expecting a threat, or for you when the police officer tells you to drop the gun and you whirl around to face him — and get shot for your mistake.

Managing tasks and processing information is critical to both an efficient response and your own safety, and that's what this drill is designed to accomplish.

The second aspect of this drill has to do with your anticipation of shooting. If the situation is such that you've got a gun in your hand, you're likely to be ready to shoot, but the point at which you actually make and execute the decision to shoot is yet unknown. Your general readiness is high, but your anticipation of any specific shot is low. That anticipation affects your balance of speed & precision because you aren't ready to shoot at the moment you need to. Understanding this dynamic will help you refine your understanding of that balance and under

How ready are you to shoot when the situation suddenly turns deadly?

what conditions it's adversely affected.

Before you try this drill you should already have a good grounding in one-handed drawing and shooting, as well as some exposure to the cognition drills discussed earlier.

## Rounds needed

I'd suggest having 2 magazines, loaded between 40-60% of capacity, and repeating this drill until both are empty. This will give you additional experience in recognizing an empty gun and reloading efficiently even in the midst of a chaotic situation.

## Target

I recommend using any one of the DT-2 series targets, so that your training partner can increase the difficulty level by making you figure out which target really needs to be shot.

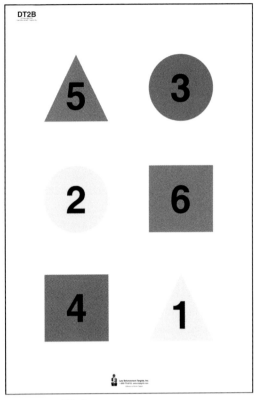

**LE Targets #DT-2B**

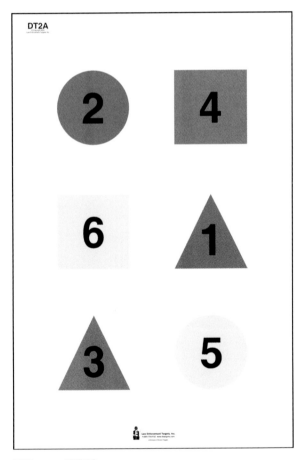

**LE Targets #DT-2A**

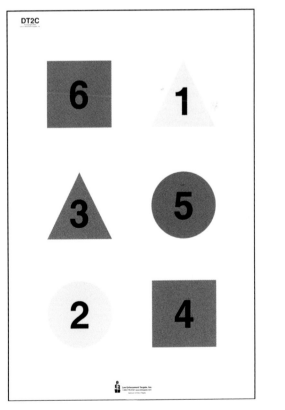

**LE Targets #DT-2C**

## Special equipment

Cell phone.

## Description

The scenario is simple: You're on the phone with 9-1-1 reporting someone who has broken into your house. As you're talking on the phone, the suspect, armed with a knife, bursts into the room.

Stand a plausible distance from the target, based on your measurements of the rooms in your house: your living room or kitchen, for instance. Carry on a simulated conversation with the imaginary 9-1-1 operator, who is played by your training partner. Make the call like a real 9-1-1 call: tell the "operator" you need the police, give your name and address, describe the "suspect" (here's where that visualization practice pays off!), where he is in your home, where you are in your home, a description of yourself, who else is in the home, their ages, and so on. Your training partner is to act like a real call taker, asking you what you need, where you are, what the suspect looks like, etc.

At some point while you're holding this conversation your partner is to call out a target identifier (color, number, shape, or any combination of those) and your job is to determine which target to shoot and then to deliver several accurate rounds into that target.

## Scoring/evaluation

Like every other drill, you're looking for all accurate hits on the targets as fast as you can shoot — but this drill is slightly different. This drill is a little more difficult than most from a marksmanship standpoint, given the varied shapes of the target areas and the slightly increased distance, and the fact that you'll likely be shooting one-handed. Add to that the sudden nature of the "threat" and you'll likely find more missed shots than usual. That's okay, because it's those missed shots that show you the effect of surprise on your ability to shoot; doing this drill two or three times (which should use up the allotted two magazines) will help you adapt to that surprise and you should see those misses disappear by the last repetition. If they don't, you have some work to do on your one-handed shooting skills!

## Variations

I've done this drill using a third person to carry on an actual cell phone conversation with the shooter, leaving the training partner free to simply make target calls when appropriate. This little change is surprisingly stressful for the shooter, particularly if you know a real 9-1-1 operator who will do this with you when he or she is off duty.

You can (and should) shoot this drill both from the holster and from the ready position, with your gun already in your hand (pointed in a safe direction, of course).

## Special notes

For the training partner: Try to confuse the shooter by occasionally sneaking in a target command that is confusing or doesn't even exist.

## NOTES

_____

_____

_____

_____

_____

_____

_____

_____

_____

_____

_____

_____

_____

_____

## Designer

Adapted from a drill by I.C.E. Training

## Purpose

Over the last few years, the approach to defense in the home has evolved into comprehensive plan: evade (get away from the intruder, get out if you and any family members can do so in complete safety); barricade (secure yourself in a pre-arranged safe area or room); arm (by whatever means you have at your disposal, be it a firearm, electrical defense tool, chemical spray, or even improvised weapons); communicate (call emergency responders to help); and, finally, respond (use those self defense tools as necessary to protect your life or the lives of your loved ones).

Shooting from that ensconced or barricaded position is likely to be different than from a standing position on the range. You'll ideally be behind cover, probably shooting from around or over something, and possibly from a kneeling position. What's more, unless you have someone in the room with you to handle communications with emergency responders, you'll need to do that along with shooting your gun.

It's a lot of stuff to keep straight, and not at all easy to do if you've not practiced beforehand. This drill is designed to give you some practice dealing with the physical parts of that response, shooting from a realistic home defense position.

If you haven't already, you need to identify your safe room — the place where you'll go (or take your family, as the case may be) and where you can secure yourself behind a solid locked door. You'll want your position in that room to be at right angles to the path of entry (so that you can see the bad guy before he spots you, giving you valuable reaction time) and behind some sort of cover. Cover, remember, is anything that will stop a bullet; a bookcase loaded with books works very well, but even the mattress on your bed can provide some small measure of ballistic protection. (The choice and specific layout of a safe room is beyond the scope of this book, and I encourage you to seek out that information to help you in your security planning. "Defend Yourself: A Comprehensive Security Plan for the Armed Homeowner" by Rob Pincus is an excellent resource.)

Once you've identified how your safe room will be arranged, you can decide how to conduct this drill. If your plan is to stand behind a bookcase, looking around the right side to view the door, you'll need to practice this drill standing and shooting around the right side of your barricade. If your room's best ballis-

**Practicing to shoot from your barricaded position is a must.**

tic protection is your bed (or perhaps a low cedar chest filled with books), you'll need to practice crouching or kneeling behind that barrier as you shoot.

For the purposes of this drill, a tall barricade can be something as simple as the divider on your range's shooting lane. If you're on an open range, a couple of stacked plastic barrels work well. Many ranges have actual barricades that are used for shooting competitions, and those are ideal. If your range has none of that, an extra target stand covered with cardboard to the height of your head will suffice.

If you need something to take the place of low cover, some cardboard positioned low on a target frame can be pressed into service. A large cardboard box, like that from an appliance, can also be used as can one of those plastic barrels set on its side.

## Rounds needed

Since this drill is designed to test your ability to shoot from compromised positions, such as over or around cover, you'll want to run it several times so that you can determine for yourself how you're going to shoot and still keep yourself safe. I'd suggest at least a couple of magazines of ammunition, shot in successive repetitions of 3-5 rounds each. Revisit the drill occasionally to keep those skills sharp.

## Target

I prefer the LE Targets #CFS-BSP for this drill, for its more realistic depiction of the target zone of an attacker.

## NOTES

_____

_____

_____

_____

_____

_____

_____

_____

_____

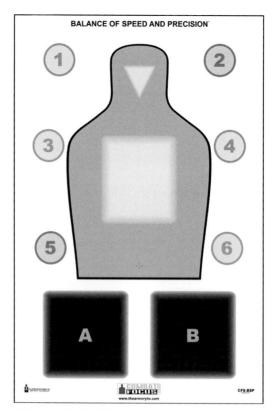

**LE Targets #CFS-BSP**

## Special equipment

You'll want some sort of equipment or prop to substitute for cover (target frames with cardboard, barrels, etc.) and something that resembles a cell phone. You'll be dropping this prop, so if you have an old dead phone or something roughly the same size that you can drop, use that.

## Description

You should shoot at a distance that closely matches that of your safe room. Measure your room and then measure that same distance to the target.

To shoot this drill, start with the gun in the ready position — close to your chest, with your elbows at your sides. If you have a training partner, he or she should give you an agreed-upon fire command; if not, you can decide yourself when to shoot.

For the first repetition, hold the cell phone (or substitute) to your ear and keep the gun close into your body with your shooting hand. On the command to fire, simply drop the phone as you establish a good two-hand grip on the gun, extend and shoot. Remember to keep behind cover as much as possible — that's why you chose it, after all — as you make your hits.

**Remember to keep behind cover as much as possible.**

**Shooting from low cover, with a target set at normal height, can result in the bullet's path going over the berm or bullet trap on your range. Check your angles carefully before you start shooting.**

Make sure you get 3-5 solid hits on the target.

For the second repetition, you'll do the same thing but shoot one-handed. This is an important skill to train, because your natural grasp reflex may cause you to doggedly hang on to the phone when the attacker bursts in. Practicing both one-handed and two-handed from behind cover is important in a well-rounded skill set! On the command to fire, extend out in a one-handed stance and fire 3-5 rounds into the center-chest area of the target.

If you need to reload, drop the cell phone and reload using both hands.

## Scoring/evaluation

I know this is starting to sound repetitive, and it is: you're looking for all solid hits inside the upper-chest target area. What you should find is that there's a big change in your balance of speed & precision as you switch from two-hand to one-hand shooting. This is natural; no one shoots as well one-handed as two-handed, but it's important for you to learn how much difference there is so that you can adjust your shooting to make sure that you get all your hits on the target. Shooting from a disadvantaged position will reveal those differences even more starkly, and you may discover that you need more work on your one-handed shooting if you're to be able to reliably incapacitate your attacker.

## Special notes

SAFETY WARNING: Shooting from low cover, with a target set at normal height, can result in the bullet's path going over the berm or bullet trap on your range! Check your angles carefully before you start shooting. If the angle is such that it creates a safety hazard, move your entire setup close to the backstop or drop the target down so that the angles are safe. The latter is not the very best arrangement, as you don't get to practice shooting at a standing target, but it's better than injuring someone because your bullet wasn't properly contained. SAFETY FIRST!

If you normally carry your gun in your home, practice drawing the gun before you get into your barricaded position. Do not try to draw the gun when you're in a cramped or compromised position!

## NOTES

_____

_____

_____

_____

_____

_____

_____

## DRILL NAME: THE WHOLE ENCHILADA

### Purpose

If you've done the Home Defense Retrieval, Sudden Response, and Barricaded Defender drills, it's time to put them all together and test your comprehensive home defense response.

You already know that you can shoot from your safe barricade position, that you can retrieve your gun efficiently and safely, and that you can shoot and get the hits you need when you're faced with a sudden threat. Now, can you do them all at once?

One of the issues in defensive training is something called "skills in isolation," and it simply means that it's easy to practice and get really good at things that are divorced from the context in which they'll be used. That context, however, often diminishes those skills if you don't understand and practice the totality of how they'll be used.

Let me give you a simple example: when I was actively competing in "tactical" matches, I decided that I wanted to use a revolver. Moreover, I wanted to beat all the autoloader shooters and take first place using a revolver. That's a pretty ambitious goal (especially when those other shooters are quite good, as were those I competed against). I could shoot as well, better in most cases, than most of them but I had one weakness: I couldn't reload my gun as fast as they could theirs. I thought that if I could just slash my reload times I'd be on even footing, so I stood in my bedroom for an hour every night doing "dry" reloads with realistically-weighted dummy rounds.

I got pretty darned fast, too! I got to the point that I could pretty consistently hit the 2-second mark (using speedloaders) from the point that I decided to reload to the point that I dry-fired the gun to signal the next shot. You'd think that my next match would go well, but you'd be wrong; I was very good at the mechanics of the reload, but the stimulus of the empty gun — the indication that I needed to reload — was my real Achille's Heel. As long as I could plan my shots, I could decide ahead of time when I was going to reload and the process went extremely quickly. The trouble was that we shot a lot of "surprise" stages and in those instances I couldn't plan my shots; many times I'd get caught up in the action and didn't realize I'd shot all of my ammunition, necessitating an emergency reload. That's where I slowed down, because I hadn't practiced the skill in the context that I needed it — when I was out of ammunition and was forced to reload.

The same is true for a skilled response to a home invasion: if you've always practiced shooting in conditions other than those in which you're likely to need the skill, you'll simply not be ready for the conditions under which you'll actually need to shoot. This drill gives you an "end to end" way to practice all of those individual skills in context.

## Rounds needed

This isn't a drill where you go through a lot of ammunition; even if you're really shooting a lot, six rounds per repetition is plenty. I recommend three magazines loaded to 40-60% of capacity, or three speedloaders.

## Target

You'll need at least two, preferably more, of the #CFS-BSP or the #SEB targets.

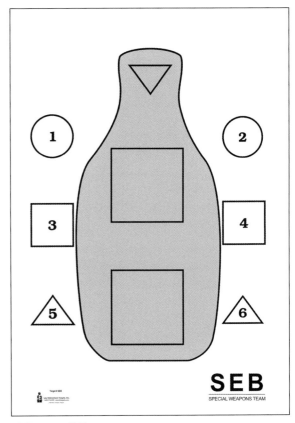

**LE Targets #SEB**

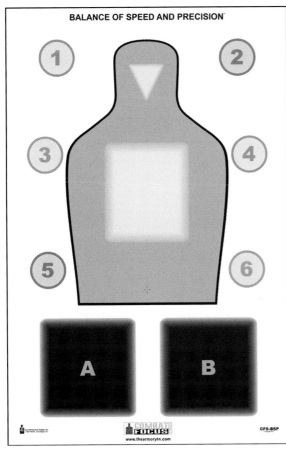

**LE Targets #CFS-BSP**

Set them up side-by-side and, using a wide felt marker or some spray paint, add some numbers and letters to them.

These letters and numbers are what your training partner will use to indicate to you which target you'll shoot. In all cases you'll be shooting at the large area representing the high chest of your assailant, NOT at the numbers or letters themselves.

## Special equipment

Since this is a scenario drill, you'll need some sort of equipment or prop to substitute for cover (target frames with cardboard, barrels, etc.); a cell phone or substitute; a quick-access safe or a suitable substitute such as a latching ammo can (if you stage your gun at home). If you always have your gun on your person, you may run the drill from the holster.

You'll also need masking tape or 1x1 sticks to set up a floor plan. The range you use must allow you to move between some starting point and your gun. It is best set up on a range where you can recreate your own floor plan on the ground or floor.

You'll also need a training partner who can play the 9-1-1 operator and make your start signal random and somewhat realistic (like screaming, yelling, or

**Set up the targets side-by-side and, using a wide felt marker or some spray paint, add some numbers and letters.**

perhaps even a board breaking to simulate a door being kicked in). This is very important to put this whole drill into the proper context.

## Description

Set up your room as described and shown in the Home Defense Retrieval drill. Remember that you want your targets set at a distance that closely matches that of your safe room or the room for which you want to practice a defense.

You'll start outside of the set, or outside of the actual range if you can. You and your partner begin by having a normal conversation; just chit-chat about the weather, movies, whatever. At some point your partner should say something to indicate that there's a possible threat: "Did I just hear someone breaking in?" or "It sounds like someone kicked in the back door!"

That's your cue to start the drill: run into the set, down any "hallways" or around any "furniture" you've set up, to get to that safe room. Pretend to grab the kids along the way (if you have any) and to lock the door when you're in the "room." Retrieve your cell phone and your gun or, if you always wear your gun,

draw the gun and get into your ensconced position.

Your training partner now plays the part of the 9-1-1 operator; you "call" and tell the operator what's happened, that you need the police, that you're armed, and the other information discussed in the previous drills. Your partner is to keep you talking and then suddenly yell out a command that indicates which target you need to shoot: it might be a number, a letter, a word that starts with a particular letter, or a math problem for which the solution matches one of the numbers. You're to figure out which target that is, and then deliver 3-5 rapid, accurate shots into the high chest area of the target.

You should run this scenario several times, sometimes shooting while holding the phone, sometimes two-handed after putting the phone down, and occasionally your partner should call a problem that is confusing or for which there is no actual target — just to test your ability to think and process information while you have a gun in your hand.

## Scoring/evaluation

As always, accurate hits as fast as you can get them is the goal. Done properly, the excitement and immersion of this drill makes it very easy to miss the target area (the high center chest) completely. Take a good look at the target: are all your shots in the high chest area? If not, why not? Were you not solidly indexing your gun on the target (using your sights if you needed to)? Did you not have a solid grasp? Were you simply pulling the trigger out of panic? Were you looking at the numbers/letters instead of the target area? You'll need to replay the drill in your head and remember what you did, then you can analyze your misses.

Much less commonly I'll see someone clustering their rounds in the center of the high chest area. As we've discussed before, doing so is really wasted time; if you can get hits inside the target area faster, then do so. Don't shoot to an artificially high degree of precision, one which the target does not demand; if you want to practice shooting to those greater levels of precision, use a smaller target that demands that — it will give you the opportunity to recognize the precision the target requires and recall the skills necessary to shoot accurately at that level.

## Special notes

SAFETY WARNING: Shooting from low cover, with a target set at normal height, can result in the bullet's path going over the berm or bullet trap on your range! Check your angles carefully before you start shooting. If the angle is such that it creates a safety hazard, move your entire setup close to the backstop or drop the target down so that the angles are safe. The latter is not the very best arrangement, as you don't get to practice shooting at a standing target, but it's better than injuring someone because your bullet wasn't properly contained. SAFETY FIRST!

## NOTES

_____

_____

_____

_____

_____

_____

_____

# DRILL NAME: PUBLIC DEFENDER

## Purpose

There are, really, two situations where you might need to use your defensive firearm: in your home or in public. As it happens there is a lot of overlap between the two, but there are also some important differences. One of those is the need to shoot around other innocents who might be in danger, or dealing with those who are running for cover as an attack against you unfolds, or even the panicked crowd fleeing from a mass murderer.

While I'd never suggest that you should or must run to the sound of the gunshots to protect other people, the reality is that when we're out in public the likelihood of needing to shoot despite distractions — and make solid hits on our attacker rather than bystanders — makes it important to train for such things.

Even if you're dealing with a personal attack, there might be other people in the environment who become part of your response. As your attacker draws his weapon and advances, someone else might walk into the scene and freeze in terror; now you have to take their presence into account in your response. The innocent person could be a loved one, or as you're dealing with your attacker someone else walks into the scene behind him. Now you have to worry about hitting your bad guy and not hitting the good guy.

Even at home you might need to shoot in the presence of your loved ones. Wouldn't it be a good idea to have practiced a little beforehand so that you're ready to handle the distractions and confusion that other people might cause?

As you can see, defensive shooting isn't always as cut and dry as you might expect.

This drill has many potential variations. I'll show you a common setup and procedure, which you can modify as you see fit.

## Rounds needed

For any particular repetition, 2 magazines will be more than sufficient. I recommend loading them to 40-60% of capacity to force a reload somewhere during your response.

## Target

The #CFS-BSP is ideal for this drill because it best simulates that upper-chest target area that is most likely to result in incapacitation.

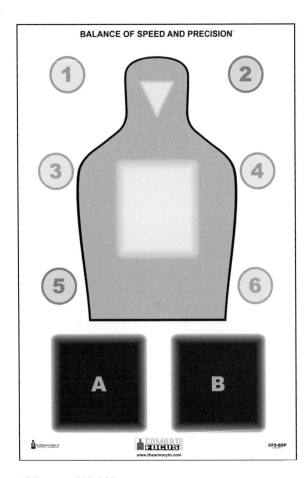

**LE Targets #CFS-BSP**

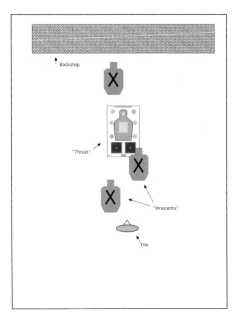

**Use the BSP target with a line or an "X" spray-painted over it to indicate "don't shoot this person!"**

## Special equipment

You'll need several target stands to hold not only the threat target, but to serve as "innocents" in the scenario. I'd suggest starting with 4 stands.

Unfortunately, this drill is difficult, if not impossible, to do an indoor range that uses lanes and target hangers. If the management of your range will allow you to use two lanes and to move between them, you may be able to use your imagination and come up with something workable, but it's very dependent on exactly what equipment they have.

## Setup

You can set this up any number of ways, but I'd start with one threat and three innocents. Here's a basic setup I use as the starter for a wide variety of scenarios:

The "threat" should be a plain CFS-BSP target, and the "innocents" can be anything else. I like to use the BSP target with a line or an "X" spray-painted over it to indicate "don't shoot this person!"

You'll notice that there is a relatively narrow window between the two innocents in front, and when you combine that with the innocent in the rear, the degree of latitude you have to shoot narrows further. Adjust the targets so that it's not impossible, but not as easy as having a threat target completely out in the open, either. You can vary the target positions to make the shooting problem easier or more difficult.

## Description

Your training partner is key to the success of this drill. You'll start with your back to the threat target. Your partner is to place you in the scenario in a different spot each time so that you have a slightly different set of problems to deal with. On the "UP!" command, you're to bring your hands up in a flinching movement (to keep you from drawing your gun when you're not yet in a safe position), turn around, and only then draw your gun and put several rounds into the upper-chest area of the threat target.

While you're doing this, your training partner is going to stand directly behind you and alternately give each of your shoulders a little push, just enough to cause difficulty keeping your gun on the threat but not so much as to cause you to stumble or push your gun dramatically off-line. It's more of a tap than a shove, but it needs to be enough to cause you to work just a little harder than if you were simply standing there.

The purpose is twofold: first, to simulate the effect of bumping into people (or them into you); second, to give you some idea of what it might be like to keep rounds on target when you're very scared and trembling. This is not intended to be realistic in the sense that it would actually happen, but realistic in the sense of making it as hard to keep on target as it might be during a real incident.

For the next repetition, your partner will position you in a different spot and start over. She may even choose to place you between a couple of "innocents" to make it harder to hit the threat without injuring anyone else.

## Scoring/evaluation

The evaluation of this drill is a little more complicated than some of the others. You'll need to recognize the area of precision that the target gives you and shoot into that area while distracted (both physically and mentally). Because of the positions of the innocent targets, you may be required to shoot to a greater level of precision in order to avoid hitting them; as a result you may need to cluster your rounds in a small part of that upper-chest area.

Check to make sure that you have all your hits in the attacker, and then check the no-shoot targets for bullet holes. If you hit one of them it's a sign that you weren't shooting to the level of precision you needed to; on the next repetition, pay attention to that.

## Variations

As I said, the variations are nearly unlimited. You can vary the position of the targets, their distances, how many there are, how many threats are present; you might even turn the threat target at an angle to limit the area into which you can shoot.

The only caveat is to resist the urge to make it too complicated, too unrealistic. For instance, a number of innocents behind the threat might be a schoolyard in the distance, but a large number directly in front of a threat is significantly less likely. Be very careful what you do; you'll get more real education using fewer props and more careful consideration of angles.

## Special notes

Training partner: Make sure that when you're alternately tapping the shooter's shoulders that you're not being too rough. Moving him or her a lot with each

tap becomes a safety issue. The tapping is intended to be just enough to make it a little difficult staying within the target area, not so much that you shove the gun's muzzle completely off the paper.

Like the BTR drills, it's a safety issue to be very careful that the shooter does not start to draw his gun until after he's fully squared off to the target. If that happens, stop him immediately; grab his arm to keep the gun in the holster if need be.

## NOTES

_____

_____

_____

_____

_____

_____

_____

_____

_____

_____

_____

_____

_____

_____

_____

_____

_____

_____

# APPENDIX: LOG BOOK

| DATE / / | TIME : | LOCATION | INDOOR  OUTDOOR |
|---|---|---|---|

| WEATHER | GUN | AMMUNITION |
|---|---|---|

| HOLSTER | CLOTHING | CONCEALED? |
|---|---|---|

| DRILL | TARGET |
|---|---|

| DISTANCE(S) | ROUNDS FIRED | TRAINING PARTNER |
|---|---|---|

**RESULTS (TARGET ANALYSIS)**

_____

_____

_____

_____

_____

_____

**WHAT MISTAKES DID I MAKE?**

_____

_____

**WHAT CAN I DO BETTER NEXT TIME?**

_____

_____

**NOTES**

_____

_____

# LOG BOOK

| DATE / / | TIME : | LOCATION | *INDOOR OUTDOOR* |
|---|---|---|---|

| WEATHER | GUN | AMMUNITION |
|---|---|---|

| HOLSTER | CLOTHING | CONCEALED? |
|---|---|---|

| DRILL | TARGET |
|---|---|

| DISTANCE(S) | ROUNDS FIRED | TRAINING PARTNER |
|---|---|---|

**RESULTS (TARGET ANALYSIS)**

_____

_____

_____

_____

_____

_____

**WHAT MISTAKES DID I MAKE?**

_____

_____

**WHAT CAN I DO BETTER NEXT TIME?**

_____

_____

**NOTES**

_____

_____

# LOG BOOK

| DATE<br>/   / | TIME<br>: | LOCATION | *INDOOR   OUTDOOR* |
|---|---|---|---|

| WEATHER | GUN | AMMUNITION |
|---|---|---|

| HOLSTER | CLOTHING | CONCEALED? |
|---|---|---|

| DRILL | TARGET |
|---|---|

| DISTANCE(S) | ROUNDS FIRED | TRAINING PARTNER |
|---|---|---|

## RESULTS (TARGET ANALYSIS)

_____

_____

_____

_____

_____

_____

## WHAT MISTAKES DID I MAKE?

_____

_____

## WHAT CAN I DO BETTER NEXT TIME?

_____

_____

## NOTES

_____

_____

# LOG BOOK

| DATE / / | TIME : | LOCATION | *INDOOR OUTDOOR* |
|---|---|---|---|

| WEATHER | GUN | AMMUNITION |
|---|---|---|

| HOLSTER | CLOTHING | CONCEALED? |
|---|---|---|

| DRILL | TARGET |
|---|---|

| DISTANCE(S) | ROUNDS FIRED | TRAINING PARTNER |
|---|---|---|

## RESULTS (TARGET ANALYSIS)

_____

_____

_____

_____

_____

_____

## WHAT MISTAKES DID I MAKE?

_____

_____

## WHAT CAN I DO BETTER NEXT TIME?

_____

_____

## NOTES

_____

_____

# LOG BOOK

| DATE / / | TIME : | LOCATION | INDOOR   OUTDOOR |
|---|---|---|---|

| WEATHER | GUN | AMMUNITION |
|---|---|---|

| HOLSTER | CLOTHING | CONCEALED? |
|---|---|---|

| DRILL | TARGET |
|---|---|

| DISTANCE(S) | ROUNDS FIRED | TRAINING PARTNER |
|---|---|---|

**RESULTS (TARGET ANALYSIS)**

_____

_____

_____

_____

_____

_____

**WHAT MISTAKES DID I MAKE?**

_____

_____

**WHAT CAN I DO BETTER NEXT TIME?**

_____

_____

**NOTES**

_____

_____

_____

# LOG BOOK

| DATE / / | TIME : | LOCATION | *INDOOR   OUTDOOR* |
|---|---|---|---|

| WEATHER | GUN | AMMUNITION |
|---|---|---|

| HOLSTER | CLOTHING | CONCEALED? |
|---|---|---|

| DRILL | TARGET |
|---|---|

| DISTANCE(S) | ROUNDS FIRED | TRAINING PARTNER |
|---|---|---|

**RESULTS (TARGET ANALYSIS)**

_____
_____
_____
_____
_____
_____

**WHAT MISTAKES DID I MAKE?**

_____
_____

**WHAT CAN I DO BETTER NEXT TIME?**

_____
_____

**NOTES**

_____
_____

# LOG BOOK

| DATE / / | TIME : | LOCATION | *INDOOR  OUTDOOR* |
|---|---|---|---|

| WEATHER | GUN | AMMUNITION |
|---|---|---|

| HOLSTER | CLOTHING | CONCEALED? |
|---|---|---|

| DRILL | TARGET |
|---|---|

| DISTANCE(S) | ROUNDS FIRED | TRAINING PARTNER |
|---|---|---|

**RESULTS (TARGET ANALYSIS)**

_____

_____

_____

_____

_____

_____

**WHAT MISTAKES DID I MAKE?**

_____

_____

**WHAT CAN I DO BETTER NEXT TIME?**

_____

_____

**NOTES**

_____

_____

# LOG BOOK

| DATE / / | TIME : | LOCATION | INDOOR   OUTDOOR |
|---|---|---|---|

| WEATHER | GUN | AMMUNITION |
|---|---|---|

| HOLSTER | CLOTHING | CONCEALED? |
|---|---|---|

| DRILL | TARGET |
|---|---|

| DISTANCE(S) | ROUNDS FIRED | TRAINING PARTNER |
|---|---|---|

**RESULTS (TARGET ANALYSIS)**

_____

_____

_____

_____

_____

_____

**WHAT MISTAKES DID I MAKE?**

_____

_____

**WHAT CAN I DO BETTER NEXT TIME?**

_____

_____

**NOTES**

_____

_____

# LOG BOOK

| DATE / / | TIME : | LOCATION | *INDOOR   OUTDOOR* |
|---|---|---|---|

| WEATHER | GUN | AMMUNITION |
|---|---|---|

| HOLSTER | CLOTHING | CONCEALED? |
|---|---|---|

| DRILL | TARGET |
|---|---|

| DISTANCE(S) | ROUNDS FIRED | TRAINING PARTNER |
|---|---|---|

## RESULTS (TARGET ANALYSIS)

_____

_____

_____

_____

_____

_____

## WHAT MISTAKES DID I MAKE?

_____

_____

## WHAT CAN I DO BETTER NEXT TIME?

_____

_____

## NOTES

_____

_____

# LOG BOOK

| DATE / / | TIME : | LOCATION | *INDOOR OUTDOOR* |
|---|---|---|---|
| WEATHER | | GUN | AMMUNITION |
| HOLSTER | | CLOTHING | CONCEALED? |
| DRILL | | | TARGET |
| DISTANCE(S) | | ROUNDS FIRED | TRAINING PARTNER |

**RESULTS (TARGET ANALYSIS)**

_____

_____

_____

_____

_____

_____

**WHAT MISTAKES DID I MAKE?**

_____

_____

**WHAT CAN I DO BETTER NEXT TIME?**

_____

_____

**NOTES**

_____

_____

# LOG BOOK

| DATE / / | TIME : | LOCATION | *INDOOR  OUTDOOR* |
|---|---|---|---|

| WEATHER | GUN | AMMUNITION |
|---|---|---|

| HOLSTER | CLOTHING | CONCEALED? |
|---|---|---|

| DRILL | TARGET |
|---|---|

| DISTANCE(S) | ROUNDS FIRED | TRAINING PARTNER |
|---|---|---|

**RESULTS (TARGET ANALYSIS)**

_____

_____

_____

_____

_____

_____

**WHAT MISTAKES DID I MAKE?**

_____

_____

**WHAT CAN I DO BETTER NEXT TIME?**

_____

_____

**NOTES**

_____

_____

# LOG BOOK

| DATE / / | TIME : | LOCATION | *INDOOR OUTDOOR* |
|---|---|---|---|

| WEATHER | GUN | AMMUNITION |
|---|---|---|

| HOLSTER | CLOTHING | CONCEALED? |
|---|---|---|

| DRILL | TARGET |
|---|---|

| DISTANCE(S) | ROUNDS FIRED | TRAINING PARTNER |
|---|---|---|

**RESULTS (TARGET ANALYSIS)**

_____
_____
_____
_____
_____
_____

**WHAT MISTAKES DID I MAKE?**

_____
_____

**WHAT CAN I DO BETTER NEXT TIME?**

_____
_____

**NOTES**

_____
_____

# LOG BOOK

| DATE / / | TIME : | LOCATION | *INDOOR  OUTDOOR* |
|---|---|---|---|

| WEATHER | GUN | AMMUNITION |
|---|---|---|

| HOLSTER | CLOTHING | CONCEALED? |
|---|---|---|

| DRILL | TARGET |
|---|---|

| DISTANCE(S) | ROUNDS FIRED | TRAINING PARTNER |
|---|---|---|

**RESULTS (TARGET ANALYSIS)**

_____

_____

_____

_____

_____

_____

**WHAT MISTAKES DID I MAKE?**

_____

_____

**WHAT CAN I DO BETTER NEXT TIME?**

_____

_____

**NOTES**

_____

_____

# ABOUT THE AUTHOR

Grant Cunningham is a renowned author and teacher in the firearms and defensive shooting fields. He's written several popular books on handguns and defensive shooting, including The Book of the Revolver, Shooter's Guide To Handguns, Defensive Revolver Fundamentals, and Defensive Pistol Fundamentals. In addition to his print books, Grant is the author of the Gun Digest e-book 12 Commandments of Concealed Carry and has written articles on shooting, self defense, training and teaching for many magazines and shooting websites as well as being featured in many more.

Grant has trained with nationally known instructors including Massad Ayoob, Rob Pincus, Marty Hayes, Andy Stanford, Clyde Caceres, and Gila Hayes, as well as local and regional trainers. He is a certified instructor for Combat Focus Shooting, Combat Focus Carbine and Home Defense Handgun through I.C.E. Training; holds an NRA Instructor certificate; and is an Affiliated Instructor with the Armed Citizen's Legal Defense Network (ACLDN) and a founding member of the Association of Defensive Shooting Instructors (ADSI).

When he's not writing, Grant teaches classes in defensive shooting all over the United States. You can find out about his courses and teaching schedule at his website, www.grantcunningham.com.